also from

aplomb publishing
San Francisco

Alfred Hitchcock: The Icon Years

Reel Horror - True Horrors Behind Hollywood's Scary Movies

Disaster in the Sky -Behind the Scenes of the Airport Movies

Curse of the Silver Screen - Tragedy & Disaster Behind the Movies

Master of Disaster - Irwin Allen: The Disaster Years

Death of a Pop Star - Tragic Endings of Pop & Rock Music Icons

Murder on the Boob Tube - Classic TV Detectives and Our Love of Mystery, Murder & Mayhem

Disaster on Film - Behind the Scenes of Hollywood's Classic Disaster Films

www.aplombpublishing.com

What Ever Happened to Mommie Dearest?

•

Joan Crawford's Descent into Horror & Beyond

By John William Law

aplomb publishing
San Francisco

What Ever Happened to Mommie Dearest?

Published by Aplomb Publishing, San Francisco, California.
Copyright 2012.

978-0-9825195-3-0
1st edition

Manufactured in the United States of America.

Dedicated to Joan Crawford fans everywhere.

"You have to be self-reliant and strong to survive in this town. Otherwise you will be destroyed."

- Joan Crawford

Table of Contents

What Ever Happened to Mommie Dearest?

One

What Ever Happened to Mommie Dearest?

"If you want to see the girl next door, go next door"

- Joan Crawford

Introductory Remarks

Tackling the Life of a Legend

While I have been a fan of Joan Crawford's for many years and a writer of numerous books on film history, I never expected to write about the legendry movie star.

There have been many great books written about Joan Crawford. In fact, it could be argued that no other Hollywood star has had their life as chronicled, dissected, analyzed, hypothesized and torn apart. After all that has been written – and believe

15

me, I think have read them all – I didn't think there was anything left to say. And when Fred Lawrence Guiles authored *Joan Crawford: The Last Word*, in 1995, one might have thought he'd put an end to the discussion. But, alas, he was wrong.

Joan Crawford: The Essential Biography in 2002 by Lawrence Quirk; *Joan Crawford: Hollywood Martyr* in 2006 by David Bret, and Charlotte Chandler's *Not the Girl Next Door* in 2008 continued the dialogue. Then in 2009 Peter Cowie's *Joan Crawford: The Enduring Star* gave us one of the most glorious recaps of a career that spanned five decades of star-stunning appeal and glamour.

A Story Not Completely Told

In 2010 I began to think that while many of these books continued to keep the allure of Joan Crawford alive, I often left them feeling shortchanged because most seemed to wind down just as Crawford finished *What Ever Happened to Baby Jane?* And all the years and work that followed was usually merely summed up in a chapter or less.

While it's true that in retrospect many consider Crawford's post *Baby Jane* career a footnote – and she may very well have wanted it that way – I felt that was a disservice not to provide a complete look at the career of a Hollywood legend simply because the films she made were considered inferior by her critics.

In fact, my own introduction to Crawford came through these very films. As a child of the 70s my first glimpse of her was in an episode of *Night Gallery* called "Eyes." and then in *What Ever Happened to Baby Jane?*, followed by *Strait-Jacket, Berserk!* and *Trog*. It was later when I began to discover, almost in backwards chronology the vast collection of Crawford's work. It was these later projects that caused me to wonder about this woman and to want to know of her life and her career.

What came from that thinking is the book you are about to read. *What Ever Happened to Mommie Dearest?* aims to be an unbiased look at the career of Joan Crawford that debuted upon the death of her husband – and the man she described as the "love of her lifetime" – Alfred Steele.

I aimed to look at Crawford's career when she realized she needed to work to survive. After surviving her husband she found that

Joan Crawford in the 60s looking every bit the movie star.

her financial picture was bleak. While she claimed to Louella Parsons that she was "flat broke except for her jewelry," that wasn't quite the case. But she was far from where she'd been year's earlier as one of Hollywood's biggest stars and the debt her husband left behind hung over her for years.

For Joan, what kicked in was a will to survive and fend for herself. On some conscious level she must have known her best days were behind her as an actor. She had seen the roles evaporate and while she knew she had fans, she also knew that a host of new and younger stars had already taken her place.

But as a working actor Crawford was even willing to accept a supporting role, opposite a host of these young actresses as she did in *The Best of Everything*. And when that didn't launch a new film career she was willing to work in television, whether it be game shows, talk shows or dramatic efforts. She was happy to be working and was desperately preparing for the day when she'd no longer have an income, but would have the financial stability to survive.

For Crawford, her shrewdest move came when Robert Aldrich sent her a copy of *What Ever Happened to Baby Jane?* The film marked a breakthrough for her professionally, and helped launch a career rebirth that would support her for the remainder of the decade. While the scripts were coming in after that, the downside was the quality. But Crawford knew the work was necessary.

And when the roles did end Crawford receded from the industry, but continued to have a dialogue with her fans through cards and letters that she continued to respond to and send for the remainder of her life.

A Tarnished Legacy

After Joan Crawford's death in 1977 the story might have ended, but her daughter Christina published *Mommie Dearest* and the book appeared to be the cruelest nail in the coffin of a superstar. And when it became a movie, a whole new generation of moviegoers was given a glimpse at the star from a different angle. Some felt is was terrible to defame a woman who's image was everything when she was no longer alive to defend herself. Others felt it was a crack in the armor of the glamour of Tinseltown. And while perhaps both are true, time has an uncanny way of healing old wounds.

While Christina thought she had the last laugh, in the 30 years since the book and movie Crawford's reputation as an actor and a star has remained. While no one intends the put her up as mother of the year, Crawford's career in film was never about her being June Cleaver or Mother Teresa.

I've been asked if I believe the tales spun by Christina Crawford's book. In writing a book with the words "Mommie Dearest" in the title it was inevitable the question would arise. And I must admit over the years, and all the research I've done on the life and career of Joan Crawford, I think my position has evolved.

At one time, like many staunch and protective fans I tried to discount the book. Leaving two of her children out of her will "for reasons well known to them" was an invitation for betrayal and Crawford should have known better. In fact, she had better relationships with her fans than she did with her eldest children. The fact that she had two younger daughters that discounted that treatment and stood by her only helped reinvigorate her supporters.

I suspect that in reality there are several sides to the story. Joan Crawford, like all of us, was human. The persona we present in our work often varies from the ones we present to our children, as do those from the one we present to our friends, our parents, our siblings, our lovers. In reality, we all exist with contradictions and most of us have actions or behavior we're not proud of. And those who know us - our children, parents, siblings and friends - know the side of us we present as a parent, a friend, a brother or sister, a co-worker or whatever role we inhabit for that relationship.

For Crawford, one also has to look at the time and place of her motherhood years. When she adopted Christina in 1940 and Christopher in 1941 she was still a top star at MGM. Her child-rearing efforts were as much a publicity stunt as they were a genuine effort to provide a home to two children in need. But Crawford the star was the center of her own universe and perhaps trying to have it all was a mistake. Especially during a period when she perhaps was unable to give or develop the skills it would take to mother not one, but two children with the special needs that adopted children sometimes come with. Perhaps motherhood at that time was not the best choice.

And while I suspect some of the tales in the book were expanded to increase book sales and please publishers, I think some level of truth may exist. And as children we often see events in much larger proportions and punishments leveled on us are often greater, before we've seen the realities of what the challenges of life can offer. Perception, as they say, is nine-tenths of reality, so abuse can be perceived very differently by the abuser and the victim, or by a court of law.

When Crawford was raising her younger daughters, adopted in 1947, her world had already begun to change. She'd seen MGM abandon her and found herself back fighting for her career and developing herself as an independent woman and artist. And she also found the pressures of career were possibly no longer as intense as they were being a movie star. Time and perspective may have taught her something and allowed her a second shot at making the right decisions. And her young daughters were the benefactors of that and of the experience she developed during her earlier years with Christina and Christopher.

In the end, I'll never know what the truth is, anymore than any-one else. But perception is reality, so what we believe to be true, in many ways, is for us. We as fans, just like her children, have had a view of her life and we can digest it, think about it, mull it over and come to our own conclusions about what we choose to believe.

I didn't write this book to document a monster, like some suggest *Mommie Dearest* aimed to do. And I didn't write it to be a biography on the life of a legend. As I've stated, many other books have achieved that. But none of those books offer a chapter on *Trog* ... or *Berserk!, I Saw What You Did, The Caretakers* or *Strait-Jacket*. In fact, most simply gloss over the last 15 years of her life as a footnote. But that's the Joan Crawford who drew me in. It was those movies that made me want to know more about this woman. It was later I discovered *Grand Hotel, The Women, Mildred Pierce* and others. But Crawford was more than that. She was a person. Complete with flaws, mistakes and things she was not entirely proud of. But those things only make me want to know more.

In the pages that follow, I'll aim to stay clear of the discussion of Joan Crawford as a mother, except where it's necessary to explain the career or the decisions that were made. I hope you find this stage of her life as fascinating as I have and enjoy the journey taken and not the destination we ended up on with the release of *Mommie Dearest* in 1978. The road not taken is far more interesting.

- John William Law

What Ever Happened to Mommie Dearest?

What Ever Happened to Mommie Dearest?

"Nobody can imitate me. You can always see impersonations of Katharine Hepburn and Marilyn Monroe. But not me. Because I've always drawn on myself only."

- Joan Crawford

Relfection of a Star

A Legacy in Retrospect

After her death in May 1977, Joan Crawford was still never far from the headlines. Her passing raised more than a few eyebrows when she cut her first two adopted children from her will and left a considerable sum to charity and additional bequeaths to her two adopted daughters.

25

When her oldest daughter released a tell-all book detailing years of abuse at the hands of her mother, the media and the public couldn't get enough of the nasty details. And when Christina Crawford's tell-all was turned into a biopic on her life, Joan Crawford was resurrected for the big screen by Faye Dunaway in a ghastly film version that caught moviegoers by surprise and brought the careful image of Joan Crawford, the movie star, to a crashing halt. It was an image she had fought long to build and protect, but the hit movie made new headlines and Joan Crawford became better known for lines like "No more wire hangers," than for her Oscar-winning performance in *Mildred Pierce*.

Since then a score of books have offered a variety of different views of the person known as Joan Crawford. While some have offered detailed looks at her life, others have detailed her vast film career. Several have attempted to repair the damage of *Mommie Dearest*, while others chronicled the men in her life and her life as a cinema glamour queen.

In addition to the host of books written about her, Joan Crawford offered two of her own. *A Portrait of Joan*, published in 1964, offered her take on her struggles to achieve fame and fortune and the toll it took on her. While far from acclaimed, the book offered a personal glimpse into her world, as she wished the public to view it. Then, in 1971 she offered *My Way of Life*, a self-help book, of sorts, that offered women tips on how to make the most out of life. Advice on how to succeed in a man's world while remaining a lady, wardrobe hints, beauty tips and suggestions for decorating and entertaining and more were aimed at the 1970s working woman, but came off sounding straight out of the 1950s. The book remains a camp classic and collector's item.

And in 1978, Roy Newquist published *Conversations with Joan Crawford*, featuring a series of interviews the writer conducted with Crawford over a 15-year period in the latter part of her life. Another title, *Joan Crawford – The Last Years* offered another look at the final years of her life after the work stopped. And she was still worth reading in the 1990s when *Joan Crawford – The Last Word* attempted to end the discussion on who Joan Crawford was and put the story to rest. The book didn't attempt to return her to a pedestal, but did try to repair some of the damage of Christina's book.

All in all, we're left with a view that Joan Crawford was a human being, complete with flaws and talent. Certainly not Mother of the Year, but far from the monster created on screen by Faye Dunaway. But which Joan Crawford was she?

The fact is that perhaps, the like the rest of us, there were multiple sides to Joan Crawford and looking back over her life and career we can see the various stages and roles she played – on screen and off.

As a child she struggled to overcome what she knew were meager beginnings and a life of growing disappointments. With little money and lack of a stable home life she longed for a father figure and for fame and fortune. As she came into her own she strived to be a dancer, not just a competent one but the best one – the hardest working, most dedicated and most willing to do what it took to make it. That determination led her to Hollywood and to become one of the greatest, if not the greatest movie star to have lived. From the early 1930s until the 1950s she was one of the reigning queens of the business. Her movies were applauded and acclaimed and made millions at the box office.

By the 1950s she was facing perhaps her greatest challenge as an actress – that of survival in a business that always wanted the next best thing – a prettier face, a younger look and a new persona. But as much, or more than that, she also longed for a life outside Hollywood. Some suggest she knew by this point that her stardom wouldn't last forever. And once it was gone what would she be left with? Her struggle to be a parent played out under difficult circumstances. Acting as a single parent

In 1969 Joan appeared in an ad campaign for Blackglama Mink.

for much of that time she found parenting perhaps the greatest challenge of all. And with a lack of strong role models she failed on many fronts, but she learned the hard way that discipline and determination were skills you needed to get by in life and tried to instill those in her children. And like many parents, she succeeded on some fronts. Two of her daughters stood by her to the end, while two rebelled and left her behind.

She also longed for a partner, and thought she'd found him in Alfred Steele. Their union was far from a storybook romance, but she enjoyed the existence away from Hollywood and thought she'd at last got it right with a man she could spend the rest of her life with. But that was not the case.

After his death in 1959 she quickly found that the life of luxury she'd been living in was made of smoke and mirrors. The money was gone and a mountain of debt was all that remained. Once again alone she had to pick herself up, dust herself off and get back to taking care of herself. It was a role she knew well, but at this late stage in her life it took all the strength she had to find work and earn a living. The roles weren't going to come to her, she'd have to find them herself. And that she did.

So, from 1959 until 1972 she worked her way out of debt and continued to keep alive the legend of Joan Crawford. And it's this period where we discover Joan Crawford – the survivor.

What ever happened to Mommie Dearest? Turn the page and find out.

What Ever Happened to Mommie Dearest?

three

What Ever Happened to Mommie Dearest?

"There was a saying around M-G-M - Norma Shearer got the productions, Greta Garbo supplied the art, and Joan Crawford made the money to pay for both."

- Joan Crawford

Icon in the Making

A Star's Life in Review

I f there ever was and up-from-the-bootstraps tale of rags to riches in Hollywood it was the evolution of Lucille LeSuer into Joan Crawford. While many such tales were mere Hollywood folklore created by publicity teams at major studios, Crawford's needed no tinkering from the MGM back office. She had all the makings of a girl from the wrong side of the tracks who clawed and fought her way to the top of the heap as MGM's number one star. From being abandon by her father to folding laundry as a young girl to keep food on the table, Crawford's was a tale of inspiration illustrating that anyone could become a star with hard work, talent and sheer determination.

Humble Beginnings

Born Lucille Fay LeSueur in San Antonio, Texas, she was the third child of Thomas E. LeSueur and Anna Bell Johnson. She had both an older sister, Daisy LeSueur, who died as a child, and a brother Hal LeSueur, who was born several years earlier. Speculation as to the year of her birth has long been a mystery. While official Hollywood profiles often put the date at 1908, many historians set the date several years earlier, as 1904, or most often 1905. Crawford herself stuck to the 1908

As a star Crawford felt strongly that she always had to appear in public made up to look like the Joan Crawford her fans expected to see.

date, the same year Bette Davis was born.

Her mother later married Henry J. Cassin and the family lived in Lawton, Oklahoma, where Cassin ran a small theater. Lucille took to the nickname Billie, and she loved watching live acts perform at her stepfather's theater. At a young age she decided she wanted to be a dancer.

When the family moved to Kansas City, Missouri in 1916 she attended St. Agnes Academy, a local Catholic school and after her mother and stepfather separated, she stayed on at St. Agnes as a work student, doing chores at the school to earn her education. She did the same at Rockingham Academy through her high school years and in 1922 she registered at Stephens College in Columbia, Missouri, intending to earn a college education, but lasted less than a year.

Her career began as a chorus line dancer. Using the name Billie Cassin she worked her way north to New York City. Her talent and determination got her noticed by the burgeoning Hollywood studio system as it scouted for talent for the collection of musicals it was churning out. In 1925 she signed a contract with the Metro-Goldwyn-Mayer Studio under the name Lucille LeSueur and boarded a train for Culver City, California.

With Alfred Steele as her last husband, Joan would travel the world on behalf of Pepsi-Cola, where Steele was an executive.

The movies were silent in those days and Billie reportedly worked hard at MGM determined to keep her studio contract. To promote the fledgling chorus girl the studio created a contest to find her a new name. A movie magazine ran the contest and a female contestant won $500 for suggesting the name "Joan Crawford." The first choice was actually "Joan Arden" but the name was already in use by an actress, so the second option was selected.

In the early days of filmmaking Crawford was cast in a variety of roles, doing whatever was asked of her. In fact, her earliest foray into the world of horror films would come back in 1927 when she co-starred with Lon Chaney in Tod Browning's film *The Unknown*. In the film Chaney plays a man hiding from the police by masquerading as an armless man in a circus sideshow. He falls in love with a beautiful circus performer, played by Crawford, who ironically has a phobia of being held in a man's arms. The two are involved in a romance from a distance because of his fear that she will discover his secret arms and an extra thumb on his right hand that is a unique marker that will show her his true identity as a killer. Crawford found Chaney "the most intense, exciting individual I'd ever met, a man mesmerized into his part."

As she grew in her craft she began to increase her popularity, her roles, and her success at the box office. Soon she was a star.

And the rest, as they say, is history.

A Rise to the Number One Movie Star

Crawford acted in countless motion pictures and ranked as MGM's number one box office draw for many years. She easily moved from silent films to talkies. And unlike many of her contemporaries, her tale of struggling young dancer without a penny to her name helped endear her to the public. She received thousands of fan letters a week from both men and women. And Crawford was known for responding personally to them all. She knew how important her fans were and never missed an opportunity to greet them in public, thank them for their support or recognize that without them she would be nothing. She became MGM's top box office star thanks to them and she never forgot it. After MGM dropped her contract thinking her best days were over, she proved them wrong when she won the Academy Award for Best Actress for *Mildred Pierce* in 1945. She signed onto a new multi-picture deal with Warner Bros. and was nominated two more times, for *Possessed* in 1947 and again in 1952 for her performance in *Sudden Fear*.

In 1929, she entered the first of her four marriages. Her first husband was actor Douglas Fairbanks, Jr. who she divorced in 1933. She married again in 1935 to actor Franchot Tone, but the couple would divorce 1939. Her third marriage to Phillip Terry would take place in 1942 until divorce in 1946. Her final marriage to Pepsi-Cola executive Alfred N. Steele took place in 1955 in Las Vegas, Nevada and lasted until his death in 1959. Crawford long felt he was the life partner she had always been looking for. He was also the only husband from outside show business.

Crawford lived most of her life in a mansion at 426 North Bristol Avenue in Brentwood, midway between Beverly Hills and the Pacific Ocean. It was close enough to Hollywood to manage her career, but far enough to offer a refuge from the insanity stardom brought. The home remained her primary residence for 26 years until she moved to a lavish apartment in New York City with Steele. After his death she sold her mansion and remained in New York where she would live in several apartments during the final years of her life.

During her marriage to Steele and after his death Crawford worked also as a publicity executive for Pepsi-Cola, traveling extensively for the company to promote the soft drink. Two days after Steele's death, she was elected to fill his place on the corporate board of directors. She remained with the company until 1973.

She was the recipient of the Sixth Annual Pally Award, which was awarded to the employ making a significant contribution to company sales. It was in the shape of a bronze Pepsi bottle. She proudly kept her

With her last husband, Alfred Steele, Joan felt she had found what she had been looking for in a partner and came close to retiring from Hollywood to focus on being the wife of a business executive.

Pally next to her Oscar for *Mildred Pierce*.

The Legacy

When she died in New York City, reportedly of a heart attack, she had been fighting cancer and knew she was running out of time. In her will, she gave the two youngest of her adopted children, Cindy and Cathy, $77,500 each. But disinherited the eldest two adopted children, Christina and Christopher, stating "...for reasons which should be well known to them."

Christina thanked her with a tell-all book – one her mother was no longer alive to respond to – and the story of an abused daughter by a vindictive and egotistical star launched a new market of Hollywood books by children of stars getting back at their parents and cashing in on their notoriety. Christina Crawford's, *Mommie Dearest*, even found its way to the big screen with Faye Dunaway creating a grotesque incarnation of the star that depicted Crawford in a light that probably would have killed her had she not been dead already.

She was cremated and her ashes buried with her last husband, Alfred Steele, in Ferncliff Cemetery at Hartsdale, New York. Her gravestone reads: Joan Crawford 1905-1977.

Joan Crawford's foot and handprints were captured in cement for the famous Grauman's Chinese Theater on Hollywood Boulevard in Hollywood. She is also immortalized with a star on the Hollywood Walk of Fame at 1750 Vine Street.

For Crawford there really are a series of segments to her life and career. Her earlier years before Hollywood came calling and before she became Joan Crawford. This was followed by her years as a dancer in theater and in film during the silent years. The third segment is considered her Hollywood years as the reigning queen of MGM and would last from the 1930s until the mid-1940s. This is followed by her independent years, from *Mildred Pierce* until the mid 1950s.

After her marriage to Steele she planned her retirement from Hollywood, but quickly found that after his death she needed to work, so she balanced her work promoting Pepsi-Cola with the film roles and TV work she could acquire. After her final film in 1970 she retired from the movie business and gradually became more reclusive, rarely seen in public during the final years of her life. She remained very connected with fans and friends through letters she received and wrote. She responded to nearly anyone who contacted her and her fans stuck by her until the end. Some reports suggest at varying times in her career she wrote as many as 1,000 letters a month, all in her own hand. She's even thanked people for their own thank you notes to her. And in the end, it wouldn't be family by her side when she died, it was a fan.

Joan and her last husband, Alfred Steele, created a fabuous penthouse in New York.

four

What Ever Happened to Mommie Dearest?

"Love is fire. But whether it is going to warm your hearth or burn down your house, you can never tell."

- Joan Crawford

The Widow Steele

The Star who had the Best of Everything ... and then lost it

While at work on *Female on the Beach* in 1954, Joan Crawford was known to spend the night in her dressing room at Universal Studios, rather than head home. With early mornings in the make-up chair and the long evenings on the set, or watching the day's rushes, the long schedule left her too tired to drive home knowing she had to be fresh for an early morning call.

43

Even on New Year's Eve Crawford remained behind closed doors in her trailer on the Universal set, too exhausted to ring in 1955. While resting a call came through from her home that some friends who were in Las Vegas to ring in the New Year were calling to wish her well. Earl Blackwell, a promotions man, had placed the call and after wishing her the best he put another guest partying with them on the line who also wanted to wish her a happy New Year. The man was Alfred Steele.

Steele was a business tycoon who started out as an advertising salesman for the *Chicago Tribune*. He moved up to an executive at Standard Oil Company of Indiana and then a manager at CBS in Detroit. After that he landed as a vice president at Coca Cola before heading over to its chief competitor, Pepsi-Cola, to be a chief executive. It was at this point he met Joan Crawford.

Joan had met Steele sometime before with his wife Lillian at a New York charity event and when he said he'd be in Los Angeles in a few weeks and would like to see her she assumed he meant with his

Joan Crawford and Alfred Steele married in May 1955 and settled into city life in New York City where they designed a lavish penthouse apartment suitable of a powerful executive and a Hollywood movie star.

wife. When he showed up single, and in the process of divorcing his wife, Crawford was intrigued. His attentiveness and interest in her wasn't surprising, but he was unlike anyone she had ever been involved with. As one of the top executives at Pepsi-Cola, he was far removed from the movie business, and he was both a powerful and enigmatic man. Though he was middle aged, balding and overweight, he had a strength, charisma and leadership quality that Crawford found very attractive. She also felt he would provide a strong father figure to her children. Steele had a 22-year old daughter and a son who was turning six at the time of his whirlwind romance with Crawford.

The relationship quickly took hold and Joan fell head over heels for this successful businessman. He wooed her with all the trappings his corporate lifestyle could provide and she found him a welcome escape from the Hollywood types she was used to dating. "One of the most attractive things about him," Joan said, "was he wasn't an actor, as my first three husbands were."

It wasn't long before Steele proposed marriage and on May 9, 1955 the couple was having dinner at Romanoff's restaurant in Beverly Hills when he leaned across the table and said, "Let's fly to Las Vegas and be married right now."

"Fly?" quizzed the star.

"The Pepsi Lodestar's at my disposal," he answered. "I'll call Luke."

"Luke?" she asked.

"My pilot. Say yes, Joan."

"The only time I ever flew was to Catalina Island in a single engine plane. I was green as an asparagus - terrified and sick," she recalled.

"That was 20 years ago. C'mon let's fly to Las Vegas and get married."

"But I have to go home and pack!"

"We're going straight to the airport before you change your mind.."

The couple flew to Las Vegas on a smooth flight and a brief ceremony was held at 2 a.m. on May 10, 1955 from a penthouse in the Flamingo Hotel. As their guests in attendance for the simple ceremony, Bert Knight, a fellow executive at Pepsi, and Crawford friends, Andrew Fuller and his wife, and Mr. and Mrs. Ben Goffstein. Also witnessing the event was Abe Schiller of the Flamingo. Joan wore a black and gold dress with an orchid corsage pinned to her shoulder.

The couple returned to Hollywood on a 10 a.m. flight the next day so she could arrive at work on *Queen Bee*, where she shared the details of her sudden marriage with cast and crew. *The Hollywood Reporter* detailed the gathering, with her telling her friends, "It was so romantic," she reportedly gushed. "We boarded Alfred's plane and took off. We went up to 11,000 feet and he held me in his arms. You might say we flew on moonlit wings ... and I haven't come down to earth yet."

After she completed filming she joined her husband in New York, around May 18. They then sailed from New York to the isle of Capri for a relaxing and glorious honeymoon aboard the *SS United States*.

Joan struggled to pay off the debt her husband accrued during his lifetime and would take his place on the Pepsi board and work on his behalf to promote the soft drink.

Steele soon returned to his vital role of putting Pepsi-Cola on the soft drink map to rival Coca Cola and Joan planned to continue with her acting career, but intended to limit it to about one film a year while she focused on her marriage, her children and her time as the wife of a powerful executive. She also got used to frequent flights aboard the Pepsi jet and larger major airlines. She was committed to a three-picture deal at Columbia and after *Queen Bee* she moved on to Robert Aldrich's *Autumn Leaves*, but was equally focused on her husband's business.

In fact, Joan's role at Pepsi-Cola provided her a new arena to use her persona and stardom in a new way. She was enthralled with the business world and the chance to use her celebrity status to promote the cola company, attending press events, bottling plant openings and executive dinner meetings to entertain clients and whatever her husband needed. She even promoted Pepsi by carting cases of it on the sets of her movies and finding ways to insert the brand into background shots on the screen. She found the role so rewarding that after a small part in *The Story of Esther Costello* in 1956, completing her obligations to Columbia, she said she was retiring from motion pictures to become "the best wife in the world."

The Steeles were deep in the throws of a fantastic New York apartment renovation, and between Hollywood activities and board meetings the couple vacationed with her children in exotic locales like St. Moritz and toured the world opening bottling plants. And even though Crawford gushed to many about how "deeply in love" she was, she also admitted the first year "was sheer hell" as she navigated her ways in dealing with a very strong man who wasn't about to let her have her way with everything. But the couple managed to work through their busy lives and marital challenges. Crawford even said "I didn't mind going into semi-retirement as a actress, because life with Alfred was so fulfilling."

Joan's mother died in 1958 and she flew back for the funeral and burial, but soon was back at her husband's side. By May 1959 they embarked on a major world tour, opening a series of Pepsi bottling plants.

When the couple ran into Joan's old friend Cesar Romero in Atlanta that May he was happy to see them but noted that Steele did not look well. He passed it off as the stress and travel associated with the current tour. The couple promised each other that once the tour had ended they would take some much needed time off and spend it relaxing together.

They headed back to New York for a brief stop at their glorious 18-room apartment on Fifth Avenue, but then were off to Washington, DC to present Senator John F. Kennedy with a citation for his efforts on behalf of the Multiple Sclerosis Society. During the brief flight back to New York Steele complained of chest pains, but passed it off as being overworked.

That evening they had a quiet dinner at home and were playing a game of gin rummy when he fell asleep with the cards in his hands. She woke him and put him to bed around midnight. That evening he suffered a major heart attack in his sleep. Because he and Joan slept in separate rooms, there was no one around to notice and the next morning on April 19, 1959 when Joan went in to wake him at 9 a.m. she found him cold and gray and laying dead on his bedroom floor. She screamed for help and then covered him with blankets and waited for the doctor to arrive. But little could be done and a doctor pronounced him dead a short time later. He was just five days shy of his 58th birthday and their wedding anniversary was a few weeks away. Crawford was devastated.

The couple had planned to leave for a vacation to Jamaica that afternoon. Instead she put herself to work tending to every detail of his funeral service which was held at St. Thomas Protestant Episcopal Church.

Picking up the Pieces

Joan planned every detail of a funeral and burial suitable for the head of a major American corporation and used the efforts as a way to avoid breaking down and grieving. "One day, I had a wonderful life and the next day, a broken heart," she said.

The couple was approaching their fourth wedding anniversary and Crawford was unprepared for what the future held. She fully planned for spending the rest of her life with a man who she considered her soul mate, an equal to her in every sense of the word. She soon realized she was once again alone, and in some ways was worse off than she was before she met him.

In going over their financial affairs should found that their financial picture was not nearly as sound as she had thought it was. They were nearly a half-a-million dollars in debt to Pepsi for loans taken out for the lavish remodel of their New York apartment, against his future earnings.

Steele had even claimed he had repaid nearly $400,000 to Pepsi,

Hope Lange and Joan Crawford in 'The Best of Everything.'

but the debt hung over Crawford from the lavish penthouse. With heated floors, a gourmet kitchen, lavish master bedroom suites and every detail a corporate executive and his movie star wife would need, the home ran into cost overruns, so much so, that Crawford even had to loan Steele an additional $100,000 of her own money to complete the place.

Steele reportedly had taken out a $400,000 life insurance policy in the event of his death, but he had apparently done so before divorcing his ex-wife, so the policy was left in her name. Crawford felt it would be inappropriate for her to fight for the money and left it to his ex-wife. While she was far from destitute, the debt he had accrued left her shouldering much of the burden. In fact, Steele's estate would reportedly remain in probate for the next seven years as lawyers unraveled a maze of his financial spending.

Two days after her husband's death Pepsi elected Joan to fill his seat on the executive board, offering her a salary and a chance to pay back the loans. Joan would eventually sell the fabulous New York apartment they had created, moving into a smaller nine-room apartment a few blocks away at 70th Street and Fifth Avenue. She would also sell her home in Brentwood, California, which she had owned for 28 years, to pay off the debt she had inherited, though she kept an apartment in Los Angeles, fully intending on resuming her career in films if she could find the work. Some reports suggest she was left with a debt in upwards of $1 million and acting was really her only way out.

The Best of Everything

Eager to get back to work and focus on something positive, Joan confided in an old friend that she was in need of a film to both earn a living and get her mind off her loss. The friend was Jerry Wald, who Crawford had known for many years. In fact, it was Wald who helped orchestrate her multi-picture contract at Warner Bros., including her Oscar-winning part in *Mildred Pierce*.

Wald was actually in the midst of producing a new film for Twentieth-Century Fox, a glossy colorful soap opera, and offered her a part in the film. But it was a supporting role, not the lead. Crawford didn't care. She needed the work and the salary.

"I'm making a picture at Fox, *The Best of Everything*," said Wald. "There's a great part as Amanda Farrow, an editor with great style. But I'll warn you, Joan, it's not the biggest part in the picture."

"Is the script good?" asked Joan.

"I think it's terrific," Wald told her.

"Then I'll do it. I'd rather have a small part in a good picture than star in a mediocre one."

The Best of Everything was the first novel by Rona Jaffe. Published in 1958 the story was centered on five young employees at a New York publishing company and the drama surrounding their lives. The 1959 film version focused on three young women in the story and their interactions in the man's world of publishing. While Crawford portrayed an older book editor who had to give up much of her personal life to succeed in the man's world, her younger counterparts, played by Hope Lange, Suzy Parker and Diane Baker, were determined to have it all. Stephen Boyd, Robert Evans, Louis Jordan and Brian Aherne portrayed the men in their lives.

The tale revolves around Fabian Publishing, where countless young working women make a living as typists and secretaries to a team of power-wielding men, and one hardened editor, Amanda Farrow, played by Crawford. Joan was happy to have the work and the salary of $65,000 for the supporting role. Crawford was cast in the role in late May 1959, just 10 days before production began.

Crawford only had a handful of scenes, but made the most of

what she had, though it was Lange who got the most attention. In the film, Caroline Bender, played by Lange, is a recent graduate of a prestigious women's college who gets a job at the large paperback publisher, but is more interested in marrying her college sweetheart Eddie. She takes an apartment with some female co-workers, played by Baker and Parker and when her sweetheart marries someone else she decides to focus on work. Drama unfolds as she struggles to get ahead and her girlfriends encounter their own woes as their lives unfold.

Louella Parsons broke the news in her newspaper column that Crawford was broke. And once again, Joan, the underdog, struggling her way back up, was making headlines. Even though the story was a little exaggerated, Joan did need to work to keep living the lifestyle she'd become accustomed to and *The Best of Everything* was her first foot back in the movie business.

But Pepsi-Cola wasn't happy with Crawford's depiction of them and complained that her tirade in the press made the company look bad. Once she realized the interview was not in her or Pepsi's best interest she put out a press release retracting much of the negativity, but it was too late and much of the damage was done. In any event, Crawford moved on and Pepsi learned its lesson that Crawford was no pushover.

The Best of Everything was directed by Jean Negulesco, whom Crawford had worked with back in 1947 on the film *Humoresque*. Back then Negulesco was just beginning his career and Crawford had a good relationship with him, but back then he was less established and more eager to please his star. This time Joan was a supporting player and he had hits like *How to Marry a Millionaire* and *Three Coins the Fountain* under his belt. When Crawford started to press him to expand her role and give her more scenes alone or allow for explanation of her character he cut her off. He did admit that he convinced her to do the film by adding a meaty scene to the script that he knew she would love, but he never intended to include. "But a script-girl told her and foiled my plans," Negulesco recalled. Crawford wasn't happy.

She also reportedly had difficulty with the movie's leading lady, Hope Lange, as would Bette Davis a short time later in *Pocketful of Miracles*. Joan was a bit taken back realizing that a new generation of starlet was replacing her in the eyes of the studio and the public and she resisted it. She fought with Lange on the set, but came out the loser when the director saw it Lange's way. In the end, a number of Crawford scenes ended up on the cutting room floor and the expansion of the role she hoped might mark her comeback never materialized. One scene was reportedly a "superbly-acted" drunk scene, according to co-star Diane Baker. Baker recalled Crawford had a tough time on the set and it was quite visible at times how grief-stricken she was over the recent loss of her husband.

One win she did get was in having her name set apart from the other cast members in the credits during the film's opening scenes. According to a clause in her contract her name was separated and had her trailer placed closer on the soundstage so she had a shorter distance to walk to the set than her co-stars.

In 'The Best of Everything' Crawford had a supporting role of a woman who has to give up a lot to survive in a man's world.

She offered to appear in a trailer to promote the movie, but when Negulesco showed up to direct the sequence Crawford was seated at a table with a bottle of Pepsi in front of her. She demanded that the bottle remain on the table throughout the filming ensuring it end up in the promo. Negulesco told her that was impossible and this was not a commercial. She stormed out of the studio, reportedly in tears.

Released in October 1959 the film was a modest hit earning $3.5 million in its domestic released at a cost of roughly $2.5 million. The good news for Crawford was that she got some strong notices for her work in the film and recognition that she still had something to offer.

Variety said "Miss Crawford users her own great authority to give vividness and meaning to a role that is sketchy at best."

Joan was always concerned about her image and as she aged she felt it grew more and more difficult to create the star her fans expected.

And Paul V. Beckley of the *New York Herald Tribune* went even
further writing, "You need only watch what happens when the camera
turns on Joan Crawford in her role of a mean, nervous, frustrated career
woman to see what the picture lacks in general. I know this kind of thing,
the woman fighting an uphill battle for love, has been a Crawford spe-
cialty in recent years, but experience alone won't explain the electricity.
Let's admit first off that the script gives her no more than a fingerhold on
the story, that it asks her to navigate in two emotional directions at once,
and to make a sudden unaccountable change of character in the denoue-
ment, but just the same, when she comes on, you wake up and begin to
wonder what's going to happen. You feel badly cheated when it turns out
finally that they're not going to let you even take a look at her particular
married man and that "rabbit-faced" wife of his. All her problems are
worked out off-stage, but even so, restricted to a few mean looks and
some vitriolic dialogue, Miss Crawford comes near making the rest of
the picture look like a distraction."

The Beginning of a Comeback

Crawford herself found the film a great comeback experience,
recalling, "The youngsters did alright, but for some reason or other I'm
proud to say I sort of walked off with the film. Perhaps it was the part. I
had the balls - but I think it was a matter of experience - knowing how to
make the most of every scene I had."

Now Crawford had to keep the ball rolling. When the film roles
didn't come forth she directed her attention toward television. She had
come close to a weekly series several years earlier, but the concept was
cancelled after thirteen scripts were developed when producers and the
networks felt women's shows were not getting the viewership to support
advertising sales. After the series fell through Crawford dismissed TV,

but when she needed work, it was the new medium that came forth. Joan took roles in two westerns for *Zane Grey Theater* and alongside Bob Hope in an episode of *Hollywood Palace*. And in between acting efforts she focused her efforts on Pepsi-Cola business, flying around the United States and abroad to promote the company at plant openings and public speaking appearances.

It wasn't until 1962 that another film role would come along, but the role was a once in a lifetime opportunity and Crawford heard it knocking even before the knock came.

five

What Ever Happened to Mommie Dearest?

"Working with Bette Davis was my greatest challenge and I mean that kindly. She liked to scream and yell. I'd just sit and knit. During the filming of 'What Ever Happened to Baby Jane?,' I knitted a scarf from Hollywood to Malibu."

- Joan Crawford

When Stars Collide

So, What Ever Did Happen to Baby Jane?

Glittering and dressed to the nines, as she always was, Joan Crawford walked backstage at the Royal Theatre on Broadway in January 1961. She was there to see Bette Davis. Accompanied by writer Chuck Bowden and actress Paula Laurence, Crawford had some arm support for the meeting she was a bit unsure of.

While Crawford and Davis were well aware of each other as two of the leading actresses in Hollywood of the 1940s, they were in many ways rivals whose paths rarely crossed professionally or personally. Davis' disdain for Crawford was fairly well known among the Hollywood set. She ways felt Crawford was more of a star than an actress, while she more of an actress than a star. Davis' insecurities over Crawford's successful career, popularity at both MGM and Warner Bros. and her success with men, as well, may have helped intensify her dislike of a woman she really never knew. But Crawford had never uttered a negative word about Davis as an actress, a star, or a woman. In fact, she longed to work with her and admired her talent.

Joan Crawford, Jack Warner and Bette Davis meet before filming.

Crawford and Davis had met before. In fact, back in the fall of 1945 when Crawford was starring in *Mildred Pierce* and Davis in *The Corn is Green*, the two women crossed paths at the Warner Bros. commissary during lunch. While Crawford's film was the hit of the year, Davis' more expensive picture failed miserably. At lunch that afternoon Crawford walked up to Davis during lunch to invite her to a dinner party. "While Joan stood there, Bette kept eating and barely looked up, and never invited Joan to sit down."

However, to Bette's credit, after Crawford won her Oscar a few months later, becoming only the second Best Actress award winner at Warners – Bette Davis was the first – Davis sent her a telegram. It simply said, "Congratulations."

Davis was playing the supporting role of Maxine Faulk in *Night of the Iguana* in 1961. It was much needed work for Davis, who hadn't had a strong film role or much else for some time and the income and acting work were indeed welcome. But the play itself was an unhappy experience for the veteran actress. She was starring in a secondary role to Margaret Leighton's leading one. Leighton would go on to win a Tony award for her performance and the play would be named the best American play of 1961-62 by the Critic's Circle and most of the praise and attention was directed at the star rather than her supporting performers. Davis was furious when Leighton received standing ovations and rave reviews while Davis went overlooked in the supporting role.

Joan Crawford was about to change Davis' life with the offer of a film role. It couldn't have come from a more likely source and Davis almost ruined the chance.

As the quick and somewhat unnecessary introductions were made – without any real or false show business embraces – Davis got right to the point. "Let's make this quick, Joan," said Davis. "I'm going to the country in five minutes."

"I've always wanted to work with you," remarked Crawford, who then told her she had "at last found the perfect picture for us to work together."

"Together?" Bette reportedly question, suggesting Crawford was "full of shit."

Crawford then gave her a copy of the book and told her about the story and the potential film. Davis was actually already aware of the tale and after Crawford left, reportedly went into hysterics, ranting about how she had wanted to buy the property herself, but that she couldn't stand the idea of having to work with Crawford in a movie version of it. She

Bette Davis and Joan Crawford in a scene from the film.

was suspicious of the enterprise and said to those present "If she thinks I'm going to play that stupid bitch in the wheelchair, she's got another thing coming!"

Davis also found out from Crawford that the film idea belonged to Robert Aldrich, a director Crawford had worked with in 1955 in a drama called *Autumn Leaves*. Crawford reportedly had a brief affair with the director – in fact, some suggest she slept with many of her directors – but the two remained friendly and in contact with Crawford often asking him when they would work together again. She had also once supposedly asked him to help her find a picture to costar her and Davis.

Aldrich was a seasoned director who started his career back in 1941. He left college for a minor job at the RKO Radio Pictures, He quickly became involved in film production as an assistant director, working with filmmakers like Jean Renoir, Abraham Polonsky and Charlie Chaplin as he developed his craft. His early success as a director came in television in the early 1950s and he directed his first feature film, *The Big Leaguer*, in 1953. He followed it with features like *Vera Cruz* in 1954, *Apache* in 1954, *Kiss Me Deadly* in 1955, *The Big Knife* in 1955, *Attack* in 1956, and *Ten Seconds to Hell* in 1959, among others.

Aldrich had read Henry Farrell's book, *What Ever Happened to Baby Jane?*, published in 1960 and had his agent, William Morris, buy the film rights in July 1961. Aldrich was at work filming *Sodom and Gomorrah* but he hired Lukas Heller, who was a relative newcomer with mostly a handful of TV projects to his name, to craft the screenplay, He sent Crawford a copy of the book in October 1961. A week later Crawford called him and simply said, "When do we start?"

Signing the Deal

With the script complete and Crawford on board, it was now

time to get Davis signed to the picture. Walter Blake, an associate producer who had worked with Aldrich on the film *Attack* and was planning on producing the *Baby Jane* feature. He knew of Davis from her years at Warner Bros. and was asked to meet with her following Crawford's initial acceptance and get her to sign. He approached her with $25,000. "We knew she needed money," recalled Blake. "So we figured if we got her to sign the back of the check, legally she'd have to do it."

Blake called Davis at the Plaza hotel in New York where she was staying during the run of *Night of the Iguana*.

"Walter who? Never heard of you," she replied after answering his call.

"I knew you at Warner Bros., Miss Davis."

"Oh, yeah. What do you want?" she said coldly.

Closeups for the dramatic conclusion were filmed on a soundstage while broader shots were filmed on location.

He was invited up to her suite where she greeted him coolly wearing a simple pair of slacks, a blouse, hair tied back, little make-up and smoking her usual cigarette. He offered her the script.

"I know about this," she replied. "Who's gonna direct?"

"Robert Aldrich," said Blake.

"Who the hell is he?" she snapped.

"He's directed nine films ... *Apache, Autumn Leaves, The Angry Hills* ..."

"Never heard of him. I bet he stinks," she responded. "Who's

While Joan Crawford and Bette Davis were never friends, both claimed there never was a fued between them and they shared a mutual respect for each other, but filming did cause trouble between the women.

producing?"

"I am," said Blake.

"I bet you stink too," she offered.

Blake thought he'd failed at convincing her but left her the script and receded from the hotel to lick his wounds and regroup. Much to his surprise, Davis called him a short time later after having a chance to review the script. Davis reportedly hoped the studio might convince Alfred Hitchcock to direct the picture, but he was busy at Universal working on *The Birds* and *Marnie*.

"I read the thing," she said. "I'll be playing Jane, right?"

"Of course," he replied.

"Who's the other broad?" she asked, suspecting all along it was Crawford.

"We don't know yet," Blake lied.

Blake knew it would be trouble if Davis found out they already inked a deal with Crawford and felt the best way to play it was close to the vest and get her to sign the check he had before telling her who her costar would be.

"I have a check with me for $25,000, Miss Davis. And I can give it to you if you'll sign on the back that you'll do the movie."

"What – $25,000 for a movie?" she bellowed.

"It's just a down payment," he assured her. "It's a binder to say that you'll do the movie. We can negotiate your salary, and what you'll get up front, all of that."

Davis signed the check that day and flew to Hollywood a day later to meet the director and work out the details of her contract.

When Bette Davis walked into her first production meeting to meet the director, sitting next to him was none other than Joan Crawford. Davis took one look and reportedly turned and walked out.

She looked at Blake with betrayal. "You've got to be kidding?"

she said. "I won't work with her!"

"Well, Bette," said Blake. "You've got to. We just paid you $25,000.

Davis had been had. She knew it and she walked back into the room, sat down without so much as a hello or nod to Crawford and got down to business.

When it came to contracts, both women worked out the details of their deals separately, with Davis expecting the star salary above her co-star, but it was Crawford who had the last laugh.

Davis signed on at a salary of $60,000, which included the $25,000 she had already received, along with 10 percent of the world-wide gross and $600 a week in living expenses. Crawford, on the other hand, opted to accept only $30,000 in salary in exchange for 15 percent of the gross and $1,500 a week in living expenses. When the film became a smash in the U.S. Crawford would earn more than $600,000 to Davis' $400,000 and as the film went into world release her profits continued to outpace Davis with Crawford reportedly making more than $1 million from the film to Davis' $600,000 when box office totals worldwide eventually carried the film past $9 million.

But first they had to get through the filming.

The Filming

Few studios were interested in taking on financing of the film. As Jack Warner put it "I wouldn't give you one dime for those two washed-up old bitches."

But Seven Arts, a smaller production house, agreed to finance the film, provided the budget was kept under a million dollars. The feature would come in at $980,000 and would take just 36 days to shoot. Warner Bros. agreed to distribute the film.

In addition to Crawford and Davis as Blanche and Jane Hudson, Victor Buono took on a key supporting role which would earn him an Academy Award nomination. Other cast members included Maidie Norman, Anna Lee, Marjorie Bennett and a young B.D. Merrill, Bette Davis' daughter, who played a neighbor of the Hudson sisters.

The story centers on two Hollywood sisters who live in an old, dilapidated house in Hollywood after their careers have passed them by. Jane, a one-time child star has deteriorated into a caricature of her former self and isn't quite running on all cylinders, while Blanche was an acclaimed actress in her prime, but is now confined to a wheelchair after a terrible car crash left her paralyzed from the waist down.

The story centers on how the two sisters are dependent on one another, Jane for Blanche's financial savings and Blanche for Jane to act as caregiver. But underlying the relationship is the car crash where Jane supposedly tried to kill Blanche one evening after drinking too much. The women unravel as Jane loses grip on reality and Blanche fights for her own survival, but dependent on Jane for everything.

The film features several key dramatic scenes for both actresses including one knock down fight scene where Jane kicks and beats poor Blanche after catching her trying to use the telephone to call for help. In the weighty scene Crawford refused to lay on the floor for fear that Davis would actually kick her so a dummy was brought in for Davis to pound on. Crawford was struck by how violently Davis attacked the dummy and was glad she didn't take the chance. She then filmed her close ups on the floor separately.

While Davis and Crawford were in nearly every scene, the feature included strong performances from its notable co-stars. Maidie Norman appears as housekeeper Elvira Stitt and Victor Bueno as Edwin Flagg. Norman had worked with Crawford nearly a decade earlier in *Torch Song*, while Bueno was a relative newcomer, having worked mostly in television, but would return to work with Davis again in *Hush ... Hush, Sweet Charlotte.*. Marjorie Bennett, Anna Lee, Wesley Addy were seasoned actors hired to fill out the cast.

In another key scene Jane is expected to lift Blanche from bed to a wheelchair and Davis claimed Crawford tied weights to herself to make herself heavier than normal resulting in back injury for Bette Davis. Crawford disputed this, but one story suggested Davis told her not to be a dead weight because she had a bad back and Crawford may have used the moment to make her co-star suffer. When Davis lifted her she reportedly recoiled in pain and ended up in the hospital for a few days.

For years rumors of the fighting and bad behavior on the set continued, but many who were on the set claimed that both actresses were actually quite professional with one another. Even though it was clear the two women never got along and Davis often spoke poorly of Crawford, neither let the dislike of one another prevent them from getting their work done. And both needed the picture to succeed too badly to let

Joan Crawford and Bette Davis in a promotional shot for the film

personalities get in the way of their careers.

Bette Davis herself said there was no feud. She went on to add that, "Like, dislike - these were not words I applied to Miss Crawford. Until we were cast as co-stars of *What Ever Happened to Baby Jane?* I knew her only slightly. Even though for three years we had adjoining dressing rooms at Warners."

After the filming of *Baby Jane*, Davis admitted "In truth, I did not know her any better after the film was completed."

The closest she came to offering a real opinion about Crawford was in her last autobiography when she wrote, "Joan was a pro. She was always punctual, always knew her lines. I will always thank her for giving me the opportunity to play the part of 'Baby Jane' Hudson."

In fact, the actresses caught reporters off guard during filming of the movie when they were overheard having a conversation on the set and the women played it up for the press.

"Of course, you know Joan, that everybody is trying to work up a feud between us."

"I know dear, isn't that ridiculous? We're much too professional for that." responded Crawford.

"Exactly, who has time for such silliness? We're much too busy making the picture."

"Of course," agreed Joan.

"You know what the word is around New York? The situation is so bad that your dressing room is at one end of the stage, and mine is at the other end. Now I ask you, look at those dressing rooms!" said Davis directing Crawford to their trailers that were about 20 feet apart.

"You know the only reason I am over there is I like to be near the cooling machine," said Crawford who always requested the set be cold.

"Oh no! I adore the cold," said Bette. "I'm liable to move over there with you."

"And we'll end the picture with our rooms side by side, fooling everyone," laughed Joan.

"I'll tell you one thing I hope this picture does. I hope it brings back women's pictures. The men have had it to themselves for far too long," said Davis. "But I must admit we had it pretty good for 15 years back there."

"We sure did," added Crawford. "But now everything is war and destruction on the screen."

According to several reports the women only had one major confrontation and it came at the end of filming. During one key bedroom scene Crawford said she wasn't feeling well and asked Aldrich if they could take a break from filming. He agreed, but an agitated Davis complained, "You'd think after all these years we'd all be troupers." Crawford shot her a nasty look and stormed off the set. Filming completed on September 12, 1962.

The Release

The feature was quickly pulled together and previewed as much as 30-days before opening and by the initial comments, everyone at Warner Bros. and Seven Arts knew they had a blockbuster on their hands. The film held its premiere on October 26, 1962 in New York and opened across the country on October 31. Davis agreed to attend openings at theaters across New York City, even giving away Baby Jane dolls on stage, while Crawford and Davis both attended a press party at 21, a New York hot spot, to help promote the picture even further. The women spoke to reporters, but separately at opposite ends of the room to avoid interacting with one another.

The film was an immediate success when released in October 1962. Within 11 days it reportedly covered the bulk of its production costs, eventually earning some $4 million in U.S. box office receipts and an additional $5 million in worldwide revenues. Davis would add that the film would eventually earn $10 million. The reviews were good, but not everyone gushed at the casting combination In his review in the *New*

York Times, Bosley Crowther observed, "[Davis and Crawford] do get off some amusing and eventually blood-chilling displays of screaming sororal hatred and general monstrousness ... The feeble attempts that Mr. Aldrich has made to suggest the irony of two once idolized and wealthy females living in such depravity, and the pathos of their deep-seated envy having brought them to this, wash out very quickly under the flood of sheer grotesquerie."

The Reviews are In

And V*ariety* wrote of the film, "Although the results heavily favor Davis (and she earns the credit), it should be recognized that the plot, of necessity, allows her to run unfettered through all the stages of oncoming insanity ... Crawford gives a quiet, remarkably fine interpretation of the crippled Blanche, held in emotionally by the nature and temperament of the role. Paul Beckley of the *New York Herald* wrote, "If Miss Davis' portrait of an outrageous slattern with the mind of an infant has something of the force of a hurricane, Miss Crawford's could be described at the eye of that hurricane, abnormally quiet, perhaps, but ominous and desperate."

Of their performances, Davis was considered over-the-top, but some took notice of Crawford's understated role.

Both actresses were thrilled to have a hit on their hands and Davis was further honored when she received an Academy Award nomination as best actress for her performance. Davis claimed until her death that Crawford didn't want her to win the award and campaigned against her. However, others suggest that Crawford was far too wise for that knowing that an Oscar win would only add to the film's profits, of which she was earning 15 percent.

Crawford did however offer to accept the Best Actress Award at the 1963 ceremony for any actress who was not in attendance should she win. When Anne Bancroft won the award for *The Miracle Worker* instead of Davis, she reportedly breezed by Davis who was also standing backstage without so much as a kind word to accept the Oscar as if she were receiving it for her own performance. Bette Davis always felt Crawford actively campaigned against her to prevent her from winning the award, but many dispute this and think Davis wanted someone to blame for losing her third Academy Award.

The film did earn an Academy Award for Norma Koch for Best Costume Design and both Crawford and Davis were nominated in the Best Actress category for BAFTA awards, the British equivalent of the Oscars, for their performances, but neither took home the award.

six

What Ever Happened to Mommie Dearest?

"I think the most important thing a woman can have - next to talent, of course, is her hairdresser."

- Joan Crawford

The Supporting Star

Time for Tackling 'The Caretakers'

As *What Ever Happened to Baby Jane?* was earning strong reviews for its stars and pulling in even better box office there was renewed interest in the careers of Joan Crawford and Bette Davis. But before its release both actresses were still looking for work. Davis accepted roles on television shows, like guest appearances on *Perry Mason*

77

and *The Virginian*, while Crawford did the same with a guest spot on *Route 66* and a role in a television film called *Della*. In addition Crawford was offered a supporting part in a United Artists drama called *The Caretakers*.

Released in August, 1962, *The Caretakers* was a drama starring Robert Stack, Polly Bergen and Janis Paige and centered on a mental hospital and the proper methods for treating the mentally disturbed. With a screenplay by Henry F. Greenberg from a story by Hall Bartlett and Jerry Paris, the film is based on the 1959 novel, *The Caretakers,* by Dariel Telfer. Bartlett and Paris co-produced the film. The feature was actually filmed prior to Crawford starting work on *What Ever Happened to Baby Jane?* with the star finishing up her work on the film around the end of June, though it would take more than a year before the film would find its way to the big screen. She was paid $50,000 for the supporting part and welcomed the money.

Joan Crawford had a supporting role opposite Robert Stack and Polly Bergen in the psychiatric drama 'The Caretakers' in 1963.

The Story

The film revolves around Robert Stack's character, Dr. Dono-van MacLeod, a charismatic, young professional who wants to validate a theory that mental patients can benefit from group therapy. But his treatments are met with resistance from the psychiatric hospital's head nurse Lucretia Terry, played by Crawford, who believes traditional methods like strait-jackets and padded cells go a long way in protecting the mentally disturbed from themselves and others. While his methods are non-violent and aimed at rehabilitating a patient to re-enter society, Nurse Terry is more interested in containing the disturbed and keeping them locked away from the rest of us.

Rounding out the cast were Herbert Marshall as the weak and unproductive head of the hospital, Dr. Harrington; Polly Bergen, as Lorna Medford, a troubled housewife who shows the promise of benefit-ting from Dr. MacLeod's methods; Janis Page, Barbara Barrie and Ellen Corby as other female patients; and Constance Ford and Diane McBain, as nurses with varying alliances.

The ensemble cast of competent actors held the film together, but no stand-out stars, aside from Crawford, drew notice.

The Production

Herbert Marshall, who Crawford knew from as far back as 1940-41 when the two worked together on the film *When Ladies Meet*, was at the end of his career and his health was frail. Marshall would die in January 1966 and would work very little after the completion of *The Caretak-ers*. For the film Crawford insisted on having Marshall film his scenes first so they could be completed as early in the day as possible, putting less strain on him.

As fond as she was of Marshall, her good will to her other co-stars was not as forthcoming. Some suggest that Crawford resented the younger actresses on the picture and avoided interacting with them. She later would have unkind remarks about working with Janis Page, who she found unprofessional. Her coldness left the other actors, including Robert Stack, uninterested in her and the daily interaction was kept to a minimum.

One would have thought she would have enjoyed working with Polly Bergen who was a protégé of sorts to Crawford's dead husband. Alfred Steele had hired Bergen to perform in a series of Pepsi-Cola commercials before his death and the work helped Bergen gain experience and exposure that would lead to her long career in Hollywood. Craw-

As a nurse who thinks she knows better than the doctor Joan wore her hair short and gray to try and look like the senior nurse opposite a host of young nurses.

ford, perhaps, felt threatened by Bergen's youth and reportedly never warmed up to the young actress.

However, being on the board of directors of Pepsi-Cola at the time, Crawford used her clout to get a Pepsi-Cola wagon dispensing the soft drink include a scene during a hospital picnic.

Crawford was interested in the subject matter and even tried to change her look to capture her role as an older woman by wearing her hair short and coloring it a silvery gray. But the star would later claim the gray was depressing and was thrilled to wash it away for all her future roles once the filming was completed.

The Release

The film did earn some notoriety when it was released as a strong dramatic piece focusing on difficult subject matter. It would earn an Academy Award nomination for Best Cinematography, Black and White, for cinematographer Lucien Ballard and Golden Globe nominations for Best Motion Picture, Drama; Best Motion Picture Actress for Polly Bergen; and Best Motion Picture Director for Hall Bartlett. Overall box office for the black and white feature were respectable, pulling in excess of $2 million in the domestic release.

But overall the reviews were mediocre at best, and Crawford failed to come off well in her part. *Variety* said, "Miss Crawford doesn't so much play her handful of scenes as she dresses for them, looking as if she were en route to a Pepsi board meeting." And *Time Magazine* wrote, "Fans of medical drama are well aware that when young doctor and old doctor disagree, the young doctor is right. So it takes little ingenuity to know whom to root for when Robert Stack, an earnest young doctor, comes into conflict with Joan Crawford, an aging, hardened head nurse, over how to handle the patients in a mental hospital... After a while,

Nurse Crawford's distaste for the proceedings begins to seem understandable."

Bosley Crowther, of the *New York Times*, said of the film, "Altogether, this woman's melodrama is shallow, showy and cheap--a badly commercial exploitation of very sensitive material. ... The only thing missing is a slinky exit by Miss Crawford, twirling her chiffons and muttering, "Curses!".... Mr. Marshall and Miss Crawford struggle manfully against horrendous odds, which even call for their being named Jubal and Lucretia."

seven

What Ever Happened to Mommie Dearest?

"If you have an ounce of common sense and one good friend you don't need an analyst."

- Joan Crawford

Anyone Have an Axe?

The Star Puts on a 'Strait-Jacket'

After the success of *What Ever Happened to Baby Jane?* both Bette Davis and Joan Crawford were hot commodities in the horror movie business. The movie legends had found they had a second act – or in Crawford's case that might have been a third – or fourth – act. After her first years as a starlet who climbed her way to the top of MGM, where she fought to remain. Her third act came when she landed as Warner Bros. after MGM let her go and she went on to win an Oscar for *Mildred Pierce*. Her foray into horror was another shot at success. She was one of the few stars who emerged from silent films with a career in talkies and she was determined to survive.

When the 1960s dawned things were somewhat bleak. After the death of her husband she found she was in need of work after realizing she was in debt. As a widow she soon discovered he was in well over his head and she had inherited his shortfall. She needed to work.

With a salary from Pepsi-Cola, having filled her husband's vacant seat on the board and as a spokesperson for the soft drink, she was earning an income, but Hollywood was the place where she felt she still had the ability to earn a living. And in 1962 she found the project that would put her back on top. It was the story of two aging actresses living in an old house in Hollywood.

All the studios rejected the project, thinking it would bomb at the box office because Crawford and Davis no longer had selling power. A young production house, Seven Arts, agreed to take a chance and the film was distributed by Warner Bros., a studio that both Davis and Crawford has spent years under contract. The film was *What Ever Happened to Baby Jane?* And it was a smash.

The problem was that even though the actresses were once again sought after commodities, the material was focused on the horror genre. And it not only opened up the genre for Davis and Crawford, but other aging actresses were finding themselves working again in horror pictures.

Both Davis and Crawford would eventually sign onto a sequel for *Baby Jane* called *Hush, Hush, Sweet Charlotte*, but before that Joan Crawford was offered another starring role – the lead in William Castle's next production, a shocker called *Strait-Jacket*.

The Producer/Director

Born William Schloss in 1914 in New York City, William Castle changed his name from Schloss, which means "castle" in German, when he began his career in Hollywood. Starting in the theater, he worked for Bela Lugosi in a stage version of *Dracula* and his early work in Holly-

Diane Baker had worked with Crawford before when she accepted a supporting role as her daughter in 'Strait-Jacket.'

wood included the role of assistant to director Orson Welles, for second unit location filming Welles' feature, *The Lady from Shanghai* starring Rita Hayworth.

But Castle found fame of his own when he began directing and producing low-budget horror films in the 1950s that used gimmicks to earn attention and pull teenagers into the theaters. Focusing on the youth market, drive-ins and double features, Castle produced a series of films including *Macabre, House on Haunted Hill, The Tingler, 13 Ghosts, Mr. Sardonicus, Homicidal* and more.

While his films were often panned by the critics they earned decent profits at the box office because Castle was able to produce them on low budgets using simple sets, lesser-known actors and in black-and-white. It was his use of gimmicks and scare tactics that gained him fame and got his films noticed by moviegoers when he used life insurance against death by fright, soaring skeletons in theaters, and nurses in movie house lobbies, to lure moviegoers in to test their wits and experience fear up close and personal.

While many found his films less than scary William Castle was even known to plant people in theaters who were paid to faint, scream or run from a movie to create the illusion of fear.

Castle longed to make first rate films that would earn him the respect of his industry and he wanted to work with first-rate actors who he felt would help bring his films up a notch from the standard B-picture horror to something more along the lines of Alfred Hitchcock's *Psycho*.

In Need of a Star

Castle had worked with Vincent Price on several pictures and while Price was a well-known name, his standing in the industry was mostly for lower-budget horror films or smaller supporting roles. What

Castle really wanted was a star – someone like Joan Crawford.

Castle tried his hands at a few comedic films in the earlier part of the 60s, but by 1963 had moved back to what he hoped would be "stomach-churning" horror. It was a production that he hoped would put

In the film Crawford plays an axe murderess who has been released after 20 years in confinement. Suspicion arises when murders begin again.

him on the same playing field as Alfred Hitchcock, when Robert Bloch, author of the novel Hitchcock's *Psycho* was based, was hired to craft a screenplay for a film called *Strait-Jacket*. It had many of the same elements of Hitchcock's hit and Bloch tried to add in enough blood, gore and macabre humor to make the film sell to horror fans. But Castle was in need of a star.

The first actress signed to the role, surprisingly enough, was not Joan Crawford, but another Joan. Joan Blondell, was initially cast in the lead. She was best known for her comedic supporting roles opposite major stars like Spencer Tracy and Katherine Hepburn in *Desk Set*, Tony Randall and Jayne Mansfield in *Will Success Spoil Rock Hunter?*, or John Wayne in *Lady for a Night*, and was cast in the lead.

Joan Blondell had not starred in a picture in some time and Castle had no trouble signing her to the role. But the director did have some reservations about whether she could sell the picture. As a supporting comedy actress she was hardly a large enough name to make headlines and she was on unfamiliar ground in a horror film. But she was a competent actress who knew her way around a movie set and would enable the film to stay on budget and finish in time. And since Castle was used to working with gimmicks to sell his pictures he moved ahead with the plan. Some reports suggest that actress Judith Fellowes, who starred in *Night of the Iguana* in 1964, was also considered for the lead before Blondell landed the role.

Blondell was actively preparing for the role and had already been fitted for costumes, but before production could begin an accident altered her plans of starring in the film. "I stepped through a glass partition in my home and had to have 60 stitches in my leg," Blondell said.

With Blondell's injury pulling her out of the picture Castle needed a replacement fast or the film would be shelved or cancelled. One evening Castle found himself face to face with Joan Crawford at a party in Beverly Hills. Another person at the party that evening recalled Castle "practically fell at her feet." He introduced himself and launched into an offer. He told her about the film, claiming he had a script "specifically written with her in mind" by author of *Psycho*, Robert Bloch.

Crawford told Castle to go on and as he explained the story she expressed interest in the project. "She is a suspected killer and she believes it herself," explained Castle to Crawford.

"And?" asked Crawford.

"She is arrested. But she's not the killer. It's her twisted daughter," Castle replied.

"The little bitch," responded Crawford, who then asked when she could see the script.

Castle sent Crawford the script and set up a meeting with her to discuss the project. Castle and writer Bloch were invited to Crawford's New York apartment to discuss the details. Arriving promptly at noon, the men were welcomed by Crawford herself at the door and ushered into her apartment after removing their shoes, as she didn't like guests to dirty her carpets. Over lunch she told them she liked the script, but "*Strait-Jacket* will have to be rewritten as a vehicle for me, or I will not accept the role."

Castle claimed the script had to practically be "rewritten from scratch," but it was worth it to get Crawford as the star. Though by most counts, not as much changed in reality. One of the changes included altering the lead character's age. In the original script she was to age from 30 to 50, but Crawford wanted her character to be younger, requesting that five years be dropped off at both ends so she would start at 25 and age only to 45 by the conclusion of the film. The subtle change was easy to agree to since no ages were ever given in the film and the alteration placated the star who was self-conscious about her advancing years.

Crawford's other production demands included a special dressing room supplied with brandy, vodka, and caviar; as well as specified breaks during filming and her usual cold set. She was also required special lighting, makeup and hair to protect her image.

Crawford and Davis Feud Reignites

Crawford's demands also included approval over both the script and her fellow co-stars, as well as the cameraman and crew. Once Castle agreed to her demands Crawford signed onto the project at a salary of $50,000 to star in the film along with a percentage of the profits if the film was a hit. And Hollywood – with help from Bette Davis – was furious.

Davis was very competitive with Crawford and saw the similarities in the roles and opportunities they were both offered and the long rivalry in Hollywood always left Davis feeling that although she was the more competent actress, Joan Crawford was always the bigger star. When Davis found out that Crawford had replaced a fellow actor, Joan Blondell, she accused her of back-stabbing and of squeezing the lesser star out of a leading role.

"… Crawford stepped in and stole the role," Davis exclaimed to gossip columnist Louella Parsons.

Parsons confirmed that Blondell was assigned the role and even fitted for costumes and used her newspaper column to accuse Crawford of stealing Blondell's part. "Then, out of the blue, producer William Castle signs the other Joan. And then he proceeds to turn his picture upside down to please her. Even the crew has been revamped, with a new cameraman, makeup man, hairdresser, costumer – even a switch in publicity man. No one involved is talking," wrote Parsons.

While Blondell wouldn't comment on the tale, Bette Davis added to the gossip column by saying, "There is an unwritten law in this town.

Once an actor is signed for a part, it's theirs until they die or drop out voluntarily. Miss Crawford knows this and should be ashamed of herself."

The fact that Davis was so furious was ironic given the fact that Crawford herself would be replaced by Olivia De Havilland on Davis' film *Hush ... Hush, Sweet Charlotte*, just after her role in *Strait-Jacket*. (Crawford claimed she never exited the role voluntarily, but that illness was preventing her from working.)

The issue eventually died down and it wasn't until many years later that Blondell actually admitted she left the part due to injury. In 1977, the year both Crawford and Castle died, Blondell explained, "Nothing was said in the papers, because of the insurance, but Joan Crawford did not steal the role. Someone had to do it."

The Movie Takes Shape

During the weeks of pre-production Castle wondered if he had bitten off more than he could chew. Would Joan Crawford be more than he could handle? He recalled that her demands were excessive and she was something of a perfectionist. But because he admired her and often agreed with her ideas, he bowed to many of her requests and the production of the horror moved along.

Crawford requested that associate producer Dona Holloway fly to New York so the star's wardrobe could be selected, fitted and purchased there. Castle agreed and Holloway found Crawford to be "a pussycat." Crawford and Holloway developed a friendship during production that would continue for the following 15 years until the star's death, nearly 15 years later.

"Joan asked me when you plan to start rehearsals," asked Holloway to Castle.

"Rehearsals?" hollered Castle. "Who said anything about rehearsals? I just want to start shooting … No goddamn rehearsals. I never have rehearsals before I shoot," said the director. But this time he would. On an empty stage with just folding chairs to sit on, the cast began a series of rehearsals for the film, running their lines and blocking out key scenes and pieces of dialogue.

Anne Helm, who had recently played opposite Elvis Presley in *Follow That Dream* in 1962 was initially cast in the role of Crawford's daughter, but when she reportedly appeared too nervous and had trouble delivering her lines opposite the legendary star, Crawford demanded she be replaced.

"Speak up dear," Crawford reportedly pleaded with the young actress. But when she failed to rise the level of expectations Crawford pulled Castle aside one day and told him he had to "get rid of her" for the sake of the picture. Castle once again agreed she was right and fired the young woman.

Crawford herself may have offered up a suitable replacement by suggesting Diane Baker for the role. Baker had worked with Crawford several years earlier in the film *The Best of Everything* in 1959 and was impressed with her. The actresses also worked together in the telefilm *Della*. She was hired for the role because she was able to work alongside Crawford as an equal and the two had mutual respect for one another. "Crawford sensed this, and together they made the words and the script come to life," Castle recalled years later.

The additional cast included Leif Erickson as Crawford's brother in the film; Rochelle Hudson as his wife; George Kennedy as a handyman; and Mitchell Cox, the real-life president of Pepsi-Cola, who portrayed Joan's psychiatric doctor on screen. Crawford also took a liking to John Anthony Hayes who has a small part as the finace of her daughter in the film. When someone commented he did all his acting with his lips, she responded, "Yes, and such sexy lips, too."

And shortly before production Castle recalled that Rock Hudson had called him and asked if there was perhaps a small part in his next film for a young actor he thought showed promise. Castle had worked with Hudson years earlier and said he's see if he could find a place for the new actor. Cast in the role of Joan's two-timing husband at the beginning of the film was Lee Majors who would go onto bigger fame on television, first in *The Big Valley*, in the 1960s and more notably as the star of *The Six Million Dollar Man* in the 70s and *The Fall Guy* in the 80s. Majors screen time was cut short early on in the picture after Crawford, as his 25-year-old bride, catches him in bed with another woman and chops his head off with an axe.

The Demented Story

The story follows the troubles of Lucy Harbin, who returns home one evening to find her husband has been cheating on her. She kills him and his mistress and his sent away to an asylum by reason of insanity as her young daughter witnesses the crimes. Carried away in a strait-jacket, Crawford spends 20 years locked away from society while her daughter is sent to live with Lucy's brother and his wife.

Crawford is first introduced in the film in a shot of her figure, legs and arms, before her face. Her character, Lucy, steps off a train, and the "Watch Your Step" sign warns us this woman is dangerous. Crawford is wearing a tight-fitting floral print dress, jangling bracelets, and a black wig with bangs that is similar to the hairstyle she wore in *Mildred Pierce* 20 years earlier.

Crawford, who was 58 years old at the, comes off best when she wears her hair gray and simply pulled back as Lucy at the age of 45, as opposed to a woman of 25 in the introductory flashback. But the look is shortlived when Crawford's character tries to recapture her youth and styles herself the way she used to look at the advice of her daughter. Castle reportedly shot Crawford's close-ups with well-placed lighting of her face and neck and in soft focus.

The main story begins in present day when Harbin is released from the sanitarium as "cured" and returns home to her brother, his wife, and the young daughter she hasn't seen in 20 years in hopes of rekindling her relationships.

Not prepared for life on the outside, Lucy has a hard time adjusting and begins showing signs she may be unraveling. Family pictures in a photo album are cut up, removing all the heads of her husband, and Lucy claims she is hearing voices and seeing severed heads in her bed at night. But when others investigate there are no signs or heads or voices chanting "Lucy Harbin took an axe … gave her husband 40 whacks … When she saw what she had done .. she gave his girlfriend 41."

Lucy's doctor pays her a visit and begins to rethink her release, but before he can bring her back to the hospital he is murdered and his body goes missing. Several other brutal axe murders occur as well leading viewers – and Lucy – to begin to suspect she is back up to her old tricks. In the end it is revealed that Lucy's daughter has actually gone insane and has been committing the murders to frame her mother and have her put away for good. As the movie closes, the daughter is carted off to the madhouse as Lucy promises to stick by her through her recovery.

Filming went well and Castle agreed to Crawford's additional demands which included the use of a sculptured head made at MGM to relfect her younger character. In addition, product placement of a Pepsi Cola six-pack appearing in the film; the along with the casting of Mitchell Cox, vice-president of Pepsi Cola helped promote the company she worked for. And Lucy Harbin's habit of knitting to relax her came from Crawford's own real-life hobby of knitting on movie sets to calm her nerves.

One issue that did arise came during early scenes in which Lucy's young daughter, Carol, witnesses her father's murder, a young girl who looked like Diane Baker was needed for filming. Castle claimed that it was Crawford who suggested Castle use his own daughter, Terry, because she held a resemblance to Baker. Castle checked with his wife and daughter and then brought her in for filming the brief scenes. But the girl was too frightened, even after they gave Crawford a baseball bat instead of an axe, so, in the end, another young actress was brought in for the filming.

Castle also claimed that one of the other difficulties he had on the film was in coming up with the proper sound a head would make when it is chopped off. He claimed they considered a block of wood and a wet telephone book before they finally settled on the sounds of chopping a watermelon in half and letting it fall to the floor. He even joked that he tried to find a tie-in with the Gillette Razor Company for a gimmick for the film, but the president of the company hung up on him when he suggested the slogan, "Go see *Strait-Jacket* and then cut your head off with a Gillette."

The Star is the Gimmick

Castle finally felt he had a horror film that was in no need of a gimmick to promote itself, although he did succumb to several publicity stunts to draw fans into theaters. First and foremost, the star herself was the gimmick used to sell *Strait-Jacket*. As the star of *What Ever Happened to Baby Jane?* Crawford could use her name to lure fans in. And with a stake in the success of the film from the profit deal she had in her contract, she agreed to tour major cities where the film was being premiered to promote the movie at Lowes theaters.

Crawford's position on the Pepsi board and the fact that the company's president, Mitchell Cox, was co-starring in the film, enabled Joan to make use of Pepsi-Cola's private executive jet to fly across country for the tour. In each city where she appeared a large bus containing 28 pieces of luggage and food hampers, as well as her maid, publicity man, pilots and a photographer was used to carry the star in high style.

At each theater well-known columnist Dorothy Kilgallen – not Louella Parsons – came on stage to introduce Crawford, who would then take to the stage holding the same large axe used in the film and take part in a brief question and answer session before moviegoers got to see the film. Once the picture started, Crawford and her entourage would head out and off to the next theater. Radio, TV and newspapers spots were used to promote the tour, earning coverage for both the film and Crawford's live appearances. The gimmick worked and theaters were filled with viewers eager to see the star as much as the movie.

Aside from the star promotion of the picture focused on the horrific elements by using two slogans. The first, "Warning: *Strait-Jacket* vividly depicts axe murders," highlighted the decapitations in the film, hoping to lure young fans interested in the horror angles and gore. Older fans would hopefully be drawn to seeing the legendary star.

Director William Castle had a long history of making low-budget horror films, but he longed for major stars like Joan Crawford to star in his movies.

The second slogan, "Keep telling yourself it's only a movie," promised to deliver a horror unlike anything viewers had ever seen before. The slogan became popular and would later be used in the promotion of several other films. For Castle, it was an attempt to play to the crowd that was drawn to Hitchcock's *Psycho* several years earlier with his slogans about not allowing people to enter once the film had started and to not share the secrets of the film with other moviegoers.

And to seal the deal Castle couldn't entirely abandon his usual gimmicks so he produced millions of small cardboard axes with blood on them and the film's title on them as giveaways in movie houses. One humorous highlight was the Columbia logo icon at the end of film missing her head.

Released in January 1964, Castle called the box office reviews "dazzling." By some standards, considering the poor reviews Castle earned with prior films, they may very well have been, but for Crawford and as most films go, the reviews were mediocre at best. Castle admitted that the release never elevated him beyond B-movie horrors as he had hoped it might and he was still known for his standard exploitation films. But reviews were relatively favorable.

The Reviews are In

While *Variety* wrote, "Miss Crawford does well by her role, delivering an animated performance," *The Daily News* found that she was "hampered by a script riddled with clichés."

Elaine Rothschild of *Films in Review* wrote, "I must say I am full of admiration for Joan Crawford, for even in drek like this she gives a performance."

And finally, the *New York Herald Tribune* wrote, "*Strait-Jacket* should be subtitled 'What Ever Happened to Baby Monster?' and there's a clue for you. [It] proves that lightning does not strike twice and that it's time to get Joan Crawford out of those housedress horror B movies and back to haute couture. Miss Crawford, you see, is high class. Too high class to withstand in mufti the banality of Robert Bloch's script, cheap-jack production, inept and/or vacuous supporting players and direction better suited to the mist-and-cobweb idiocies of the Karloff school of suspense."

Bosley Crowther of *The New York Times* was unimpressed after seeing the film in January 1964, writing, "The story is utterly invalid, psychologically and dramatically, and William Castle's direction and production are on the cheapest, sleaziest side. The only conceivable audience for this piece of melodramatic rot is those who have a taste for ghoulish violence and blunt shock-effected thrills."

Joan Crawford appeared onstage at theaters to promote the film carrying an axe.

One of Crawford's most pleasing results of the film was that following *What Ever Happened to Baby Jane?*, Bette Davis also made a horror release around the same time as *Strait-Jacket*. And of the two features, the Joan Crawford film fared better at the box office. Most claimed that it was due to Crawford's live appearances to promote the film rather than the film being better than Davis' *Dead Ringer*. Bette Davis remarked, "She criticized me for raffling off dolls on stage for *Baby Jane* and she got a goddamn axe under her skirt!"

eight

What Ever Happened to Mommie Dearest?

"If I can't be me, I don't want to be anybody. I was born that way."
- Joan Crawford

Battling Bette Davis

Hush ... Hush, Miss Crawford

Joan Crawford was the queen of MGM and for many years a number one box office star in Hollywood. She was a star that at times shined brighter than any in Tinseltown. Bette Davis, on the other hand, was the queen of Warner Bros. While her stardom might not have been as lustrous as Crawford's, she was considered the more accomplished actress of the two, whose talent would earn her an Academy Award in 1935 for *Dangerous* and in 1938 for *Jezebel*. Crawford finally landed her own Oscar for *Mildred Pierce* in 1945, and would be nominated two additional times. By then the two women were considered fierce competitors. While they each shared some admiration for the other – their desire to be the better actress and the bigger star made a battle that some suggest would pit the two against one another for their entire careers and the better part of both their lives.

By the 1950s both actresses were struggling for survival in Hollywood. As they aged starlets like Marilyn Monroe, Elizabeth Taylor, Grace Kelly and Doris Day were getting the leading lady treatment and every role that came their way required aging actresses like Crawford or Davis to prove themselves as box office draws. For the public was always looking for the next best thing.

Davis had stepped away from the business in the early 1950s to focus on family, maintaining her marriage and raising children. She didn't work much during the decade and some say she was content trying to be a good wife and mother. Others suggest she knew the roles were growing fewer and farther between and figured her willingness to step away from the big screen showed she left by her own choice, not by the choice of the movie makers or the public.

Crawford, on the other hand had left MGM and moved to Warner Bros. only to win an Oscar. During the early 50s she was still riding high with films like *Johnny Guitar, Sudden Fear, Female on the Beach* and *Queen Bee*. But in May 1955 she married for the fourth and final time to Alfred Steele, chairman of the board for Pepsi-Cola. With four children and a new husband who had a powerful and successful career of his own away from Hollywood, Crawford too began to see a life outside Hollywood. As the wife of an executive she could travel with him and promote Pepsi-Cola using her celebrity status. She too began to look less at making movies and more at making a life for herself. She relocated to New York and designed a Manhattan apartment suitable for a high-powered executive and a movie star.

However, both Davis and Crawford were on a collision course of sorts and fate would not allow them to live the lives of happily married wives and mothers. Bette Davis' daughter was diagnosed as mentally disabled in 1954 and while the care was time consuming and difficult it could also be expensive. She returned to work in *The Virgin Queen* and

Joan Crawford found one film with Bette Davis was enough.

next in *Storm Center*, but the roles were not as glamorous and not as easy to come by and she worked only periodically. By the time her marriage fell apart in 1959 she had to return to the stage for work. Hollywood was less than interested.

For Crawford, she performed in a few features as well during these times, *Autumn Leaves* and *The Story of Esther Costello* offered suitable roles for a woman her age, but the movies were not as big or lustrous as they had been. And that was okay until May 1959 when her husband dropped dead of a heart attack. It was difficult enough losing the man she had hoped to spend the rest of her life with, but what was worse was the fact that he left her with a mountain of debt from loans he had taken out from Pepsi-Cola. "I haven't a nickel. Only my jewels," she told gossip columnist Louella Parsons. "His company did not reimburse me for the half-million dollars I spent on the apartment."

With both actresses without husbands, they became single working mothers and while that bond might have been something they could have shared, there was little love lost between Bette Davis and Joan Crawford.

However, even without a fondness for one another, Crawford and Davis had a mutual respect for one another and a certain level of envy. Davis always seemed to dislike Crawford, but admired her stardom and beauty and the men she acquired along the way. On the other hand Crawford longed for the respect and admiration of her peers for her acting ability and always though Davis was a first rate talent - A talent she actually hoped to work with one day professionally.

Working Actresses

After a small cameo role in Jerry Wald's production of *The Best of Everything*, Crawford returned to Hollywood in 1959, but retained her husband's seat on the Pepsi board and would continue as a spokesperson for the soft drink.

Davis also needed work, but rejected a role in *The Unforgiven* saying "I turned it down. I'll be damned if I play Burt Lancaster's mother after 30 years in the business."

But desperate times call for desperate measures and finally Davis gave in to a support role as Apple Annie, a homeless woman who

Joan was fitted for costumes as cousin Miriam for the film.

sells apples to Glenn Ford and Hope Lange in *Pocketful of Miracles*. The Frank Capra film would offer a small part to Davis and she hated doing the film, but the paycheck was all she was after. "I should never have come back to Hollywood," she said in 1976. "I hate all of you! And Apple Annie most of all. I must have been out of my mind to come back here."

Crawford had been looking for a suitable film for her and Davis and *What Ever Happened to Baby Jane?* proved to be the success they were looking for, re-launching the careers of both actresses.

The success of the film became a blessing and a curse for both Crawford and Davis, as well as a number of other aging actresses because it launched what some called a Grand Guignol period for Hollywood horror.

The success of *What Ever Happened to Baby Jane?* would lead to a host of similar films putting legendary actresses in harms way in cheap gruesome horror films. In addition to Crawford and Davis, actresses like Barbara Stanwyck, Olivia De Havilland, Shelly Winters, Lana Turner, Debbie Reynolds and Anne Southern would take part in similar films.

With the hit bringing new life to the careers of Davis and Crawford it was quickly suggested that the pair continue with another film that could act as a sequel of sorts. Originally called "What Ever Happened to Cousin Charlotte?" the feature was later renamed *Hush, Hush ... Sweet Charlotte* so it wouldn't be considered a sequel to the original. While the tale held many similar elements the story would take place in New Orleans and pit cousins against one another in a dark and dreary mansion where murder and lies seem to be all that's left.

Crawford had suffered a difficult time on the set of *What Ever Happened to Baby Jane?* with Davis looking down on her and creating an atmosphere that Crawford found difficult to work in. Though the women were professional with each other on the set Davis never hid her personal dislike for her co-star and rarely had anything but negative comments about her as a person or as an actress. "Joan and I have never been warm friends," Davis once said. I admire her, yet I feel uncomfortable with her. To me she is the personification of the Movie Star. I have always felt her greatest performance is Crawford being Crawford."

When *Hush, Hush ... Sweet Charlotte* came about Crawford immediately saw the profits the film would bring her and the continued chance to remain a star on the big screen, but once on set and faced with daily combat with Davis, the situation began to get out of hand.

After earning an Oscar nomination for her performance in *Baby Jane*, Davis was still angry at Crawford because she suspected she worked against her trying to get industry insiders to prevent her from winning her third Academy Award. And on Oscar night when the awards

Joan in an early scene for the film she filmed with Cecil Kellaway.

were given out Crawford offered to stand in to accept any actress award if a participant was not in attendance. When Anne Bancroft won the award for *The Miracle Worker* it was Crawford who got to accept on her behalf walking past Bette Davis and onto the stage to accept the award with honor. The incident incensed Davis and on the set of *Hush, Hush ... Sweet Charlotte* Davis worked overtime to turn cast and crew against Crawford and making her feel like an outsider for a film she helped bring to life.

Davis didn't want Crawford in the film. Though the two claimed never to have a fued, they never claimed to be friends either. Davis didn't want to share the screen with her again, but only agreed because it was what the studio wanted. And Fox was funding the film - and ultimately Davis' salary. There were rumors that Davis agreed to co-star with Crawford if they could film their scenes separately, each with a stand-in for the other and the editors could splice together the footage. However, this was not the case and no director or producer would have accepted the demand. Some suggest the rumor came from a joke Davis made prior to filming.

The original screenplay was by Henry Farrell, who had been the author of the novel on which *Baby Jane* was based. But Farrell was replaced with Lukas Heller, the man who had turned Farrell's *What Ever Happened to Baby Jane?* novel into a screenplay. Davis was reportedly upset with the change and Crawford wasn't pleased with the resulting script.

A Not-So Hasty Exit

With a budget of about $1.3 million, shooting began on location in Baton Rouge in on June 4, 1964, but Bette Davis only filmed one scene with Crawford. In the opening sequence when Davis watches

Crawford's character arrive by taxing and enter her aged Louisiana mansion, Crawford and Davis acted together without exchanging a line. No other footage of the two women together was completed. *Life* magazine, however, did have a photographer shoot photos of the two stars together, posed sitting on two gravestones, but the photos were never published in the magazine, since Crawford failed to complete the picture.

Co-stars in *Charlotte* included Victor Bueno, who was familiar from his work in *Baby Jane*, and Barbara Stanwyck was cast in the role of the slovenly housekeeper Velma, but Stanwyck exited the role before filming and Agnes Moorehead was cast in the part which would lead to an Oscar nomination as best supporting actress. For Stanwyck it left her with a contractual obligation for a film and she was reportedly forced to make the 1964 movie *Roustabout* with Elvis Presley.

Crawford, in turn, took ill during the filming and quickly brought the production to a halt. At first they tried to shoot around her, using her stand-in or filming scenes she was not a part of, but soon that became difficult. After two weeks in the hospital the film temporarily shut down at the end of June 1964. Crawford returned to the set on July 20, but could only work sporadically due to her weakened state. "She [Davis] wanted to make a basket case out of Joan, and she almost succeeded" said director George Cukor, who was a friend of Crawford's.

According to Motion Picture magazine at key scenes for Crawford Bette Davis positioned herself on the set directly in line with the camera and within the actress' line of sight. And during one of Crawford's close-ups Davis was heard saying "You're not going to let her do it like that, are you?"

When the production moved to Los Angeles for the studio interiors, a delay occurred when Davis was called away for re-shoots on *Where Love Has Gone,* but by the time she was back Crawford took ill again.

By the end of July production shut down again to give Joan a chance to fully recover, but by August 4, Crawford was back under doctor's care and unable to work and the film shut down indefinitely. Some suggest that the fact that her character is killed by Davis' Charlotte in the climax of the film was one element Crawford found hard to take. But the story required it and some speculation was made that she failed to finish a film that allowed Bette Davis to "finish her," although it wasn't all that different from *What Ever Happened to Baby Jane?*

Davis was beside herself with anger at Crawford's continued absence and quickly began to push to replace Crawford. Soon the producers began approaching other actors to take her place. Katherine Hepburn refused, as did Vivien Leigh. "I can just about stand looking at Joan Crawford's face at six-o'clock in the morning, but not Bette Davis." said Leigh in turning down the role.

Olivia DeHavilland was at last approached and she too rejected the film but after personal pleas from Davis she finally agreed to take

A shot for 'Life' magazine that never appeared in print.

part. "I heard the news of my replacement over the radio, lying in my hospital bed," recalled Crawford. "I wept for 39 hours."

The Release

Coming in at a budget near $2 million, the film reportedly grossed $7 million compared to *What Ever Happened to Baby Jane?* Which cost less than $1 million cost and a gross of more than $9 million. Some have suggested had Davis put the film first and worked with Crawford the film would have fared better at the box office and cost much less, possibly exceeding *Baby Jane's* with the two stars reunited.

The *New York Times* called the film "grossly contrived, purposely sadistic, and brutally sickening ... grisly pretentious, disgusting and profoundly annoying.... Davis accomplishes a straight melodramatic tour de force. Moorehead is allowed to get away with some of the broadest mugging and snarling ever done by a respectable actress ... deHavilland is closer to normal."

Crawford though upset at being replaced, but was also in some ways relieved at finally being done with Bette Davis, some suggest. She had longed to work with the veteran actress and finally got her chance, but it was a heavy price to pay. And for both Crawford and Davis the bulk of their work in their later years would resemble versions of *Baby Jane*.

What Ever Happened to Mommie Dearest?

nine

What Ever Happened to Mommie Dearest?

"I love playing bitches. There's a lot of bitch in every woman - a lot in every man."

- Joan Crawford

Seeing is Believing

Castle and Crawford Re-Team for 'I Saw What You Did'

After Joan Crawford starred in William Castle's *Strait-Jacket* in 1964, Castle followed it up with another shocker for another legendary leading lady – Barbara Stanwyck, but he wasn't done with Crawford just yet. While *The Night Walker* put Stanwyck front and center as the star of the film, she wasn't thrilled with the experience or the final result. In fact she opted to step away from making feature films, focusing more on television, rather than accept roles "where a mother eats her young" as she once commented about types of films she was being offered.

For Castle's next effort, the script was clearly aimed at the teen-

Although she wasn't the star of the picture and dies roughly halfway through, Crawford received top billing in 'I Saw What You Did.'

age market and much more along the lines of *Strait-Jacket*. And while Castle didn't want to mess with a good thing, he felt again a star name would add a level of civility to the film. The problem was the story was centered on two teenage girls.

I Saw What You Did is based on a novel by Ursula Curtiss that tells the story of a pair of young girls who get in over their head while making crank telephone calls to numbers in the phone book and telling the person on the other end, "I know who you are and I saw what you did." The game seems harmless enough and provides a simple pastime until the girls use the line on a killer who then sets out on finding them and getting rid of his so-called witnesses.

The Casting

Castle purchased the film rights to the story and hired William McGivern to craft it into a screenplay. In the roles of the girls he hired two unknown teenagers who had little acting experience. Andi Garrett and Sara Lane were high school students the director chose for the film. Garrett portrayed Libby Mannering, while Lane took the part of her best friend Kit Austin. Libby's younger sister, Tess, was played by Sharyl Locke and the killer was played by John Ireland. Parents of two of the girls were played by Leif Erikson and Pat Breslin. Beslin had worked with Castle several years earlier in another horror called *Homicidal*, while Erickson had recently starred alongside Crawford in *Strait-Jacket*. But they were not the only cast members with whom the director had worked with before.

Castle claimed that Universal allowed him to cast unknowns in the starring roles provided he could get an A-list star name in a cameo supporting role. Similar to the role Janet Leigh played in *Psycho*, the star would exit the film early, but the name on the marquee would help generate buzz and interest in the film. Castle immediately thought of Joan Crawford. Crawford was reportedly offered the role of Amy one month after having been fired from *Hush, Hush ... Sweet Charlotte.*

Castle said he asked the star to do the film as a favor to him and she agreed. However, reports suggest that Crawford agreed to do the film for several reasons. First, it was agreed that she would be paid the same amount as she earned on *Strait-Jacket,* even though her role was a small one. She also agreed on the condition that she received star billing on the picture so the role wouldn't impact her career in any negative way in the future. Castle agreed to both demands.

Castle reportedly started a rumor in the press that Crawford was put into the role only to be killed off early on because the director could not afford to pay her to star in the entire film. Crawford in fact is in relatively few scenes in the picture and is killed off early and she claimed the part was designed for her much in the way Alfred Hitchcock utilized

Andi Garrett and Sara Lane play teenagers in the film.

Janet Leigh as the star of *Psycho* only to kill her off early in the story. She completed her scenes in four days of filming.

Director George Cukor, longtime friend of Crawford's suggested that she wanted to believe in the success of the film and to keep working at her craft. "Of course she rationalized what she did," recalled Cukor. "She would write to me about these pictures, actually believing that they were quality scripts. You could never tell her that they were garbage. She was a star, and this was her next picture."

Joan in costume on the set of 'I Saw What You Did.'

The Production

Crawford had worked with co-star John Ireland more than a decade earlier in her film *Queen Bee* and it would be familiar ground starring opposite him. In fact, the two reportedly had an affair while making the 1950s drama. Castle himself claimed that the telephone was the actual star of the picture.

To get the young stars prepared for their roles the director said he had them to make similar calls themselves. "I allowed them to actually make several crank calls a day from numbers I picked at random out of the phone book. To experience the actual results, they improvised the calls getting a sense of reality which they would later translate to the screen," he said.

Castle had worked his formula into a finely-tuned machine. His

Joan Crawford and John Ireland co-starred in the film and had worked before in 'Queen Bee' roughly a decade earlier.

horror films were crafted with certain elements inserted to provide the shocks, twists and turns needed to keep the story rolling along until the climactic finale.

I Saw What You Did had all the elements of a Castle picture and in many ways was a culmination of his years of experience in Hollywood. Being able to produce the film on a small budget yet have name actors like Joan Crawford above the title came from years of experience and contacts and enabled him to follow each picture with the next.

A Horror for Teens

A catchy, cute 60s pop music theme kicks off the motion picture as Libby, on split screen with Kit, her best friend are planning a night of fun as her parents are out for the evening. The title credits roll and then the story begins with Libby's parents giving her instructions for being careful and watching her younger sister after the baby sitter cancels. The teenage girls assure them they can handle things and the adults head off until the close of the picture.

Dave and Ellie Mannering are off on an overnight business trip to Santa Barbara, 90 miles away from their farmhouse in the country. With the baby sitter ill, they reluctantly leave nine-year-old Tess and teenage sister Libby home alone. Libby's friend Kit joins them.

After a tour of the house the girls begin their games of telephone crank calling and come across a man named Steve Marak, who is about to murder his wife. When the wife, played by Joyce Meadows, enters the bathroom to shout at her husband, Castle does a twist on *Psycho* and has Marak, the killer in the shower, he opens the door and pulls her in and stabs her to death, finally pushing her through a glass shower door for a shocking end.

While he's killing his wife the girls are calling him, but they give up when he fails to answer the phone, but mark the page intending to call him back later. The commotion causes Marak's nosey neighbor named Amy, portrayed by Crawford, to venture over to see what has happened. Marak claims he stumbled in the shower and broke the glass and tells Amy his wife has left him. He manages to get rid of Amy and then gets the body out of the house and disposes of it in a nearby wooded area.

Amy, who has her sights set on Steve, returns to make a move for him, but the telephone rings again and the girls are calling back, this time telling him they "know who he is and saw what he did." Amy

Even though she was killed midway through the picture, Joan was featured heavily in the promotion of the William Castle film in order to draw in older filmgoers. Younger audiences were drawn to the horror aspects of the film.

overhears part of the conversation and suspects Steve is having an affair, while Steve tries to find out who the caller is, thinking they have seen him dispose of his wife's body. Amy, in the meantime, discovers the bloody bathroom and begins to suspect foul play.

Later, the girls venture out in the car to Steve's address, which they get from the phone book, because they are curious about him. Steve catches Libby peering into his window and heads out to kill her, but before he can Amy appears and pushes the girl away. She tells Libby she's "too young," but takes her car registration to threaten her.

The girls drive off and Amy returns to Steve telling him she's figured out everything, including his wife's murder and attempts to blackmail Steve into marrying her. Steve stabs Amy to death in a dramatic confrontation and Steve uses the car registration to head off and find his witnesses before they go to the police.

Kit's father picks her up from the Mannerings and a radio broadcast about a killer comes across in the car and she confesses to her father and the police arrive in time to save Libby and her sister Tess from the killer. As the adults arrive the credits roll.

William Castle uses mist around the dark and large farmhouse, and slamming of doors to add suspense. He also pulls out other traditional horror movie tricks, including his rip-off shower scene of *Psycho*, to scare moviegoers.

Reviews were mediocre at best. In theaters in July 1965, a tag line to promote the film suggested, "Fate dials the number ... terror answers the phone!"and "You may be the target ... of the next phone call..."

Variety called the film a "well-produced, well-acted entry in the suspense-terror field. Miss Crawford's role is well handled, and vital to the story. Slightest gesture or expression of this veteran conveys vivid emotion."

The New York Times called the feature "a generally broad and belabored expansion of a nifty idea." And the review added that "the picture would have brightened and chilled considerably more minus about half an hour, with the entire story held to the impressionable viewpoint of the youngsters. Unfortunately [Castle] dawdles the tempo. And the middle chapter involving Ireland and Miss Crawford is redundant."

And finally, *Time* magazine said the film "delivers its message by telephone, and rings in some crude but effective suspense.... Joan is given big billing but has a small role, and soon both her number and her time are up. The plot perks right along without her.... Any who are hooked on horror shows will find every reason to haunt Castle's."

ten

What Ever Happened to Mommie Dearest?

"Hollywood is like life, you face it with the sum total of your equipment."

- Joan Crawford

A Star Goes 'Berserk!'

Joan Crawford Heads to England and the Circus for Murder

In 1965 Pepsi-Cola merged with Frito-Lay to become PepsiCo. While the new brand retained a strong hold on its history and the brand focused on the soft drink as a core product it was also looking ahead. Debuting Diet Pepsi and Mountain Dew, it knew keeping a foothold in present day modern culture was vital to its future. By 1967 they were pushing a new marketing campaign, "Come

131

Alive! You're in the Pepsi Generation" and the days of Joan Crawford as a spokesperson for the soft drink were numbered. Her clout in Hollywood had faded and her ties to company. and the new, youthful generation they were after, failed to exist.

And while her work promoting the brand was diminishing she lacked the desired to putter about at home in her New York apartment and longed to keep busy. In fact, with the movie roles fewer and father between and her Pepsi income less than stellar, Joan sold her New York apartment she had moved to after the death of her husband Alfred Steele. She didn't really require that much space and expense and opted for a small, less expensive apartment at 69th and Lexington, remaining in New York City. But what she really needed was a movie role in Hollywood.

Joan with producer Herman Cohen during the filming of "Berserk' in London.

She managed to find some work in television, but it was far from the leading roles of a movie star. She found work in an extended episode of *The Man from Uncle* called "The Karate Killers," which aired in April 1967, but it was merely a cameo role. Her others efforts centered on appearances as herself on episodes of *The Hollywood Palace, What's My Line, To Tell the Truth, Girl Talk,* as a presenter on The Academy Awards and various other talks shows and game show appearances.

For Crawford, every appearance was her next major role and she took them all with the utmost seriousness and approached them equally with professionalism and as an opportunity to reach her public – the fans who stuck by her through thick and thin, but what she really wanted was a film. And Herman Cohen was about to present her with an offer she wouldn't refuse.

The Star's Producer

Herman Cohen was a B-movie producer who started out as an usher at the Dexter Theater in Detroit, Michigan when he was just 12. Like William Castle, Cohen worked his way up in the business from his humble beginnings – first to manager of the Dexter by the time he was 18 and then as assistant manager of the larger Fox Theater. From there he became a sales manager for Columbia Pictures working as a regional representative in Detroit until he headed west to work in Columbia's publicity department in the 1940s.

By the 1950s Cohen was producing films, first working as assistant for Jack Broder and Realart Pictures on films like *Bride of the Gorilla, Battles of Chief Pontiac*, and *Bela Lugosi Meets a Brooklyn Gorilla*. And after stints at Allied Artists and United Artists producing films like *Target Earth, Magnificent Roughnecks* and *Crime of Passion*, he began focusing more on his own efforts. Cohen wrote screenplays for at least nine films, often co-writing with friend and collaborator Aben Kandel. One such screenplay was for a film called *Circus of Blood*. It was a horror story that centered on a series of murders at a circus and the star was a mistress of the ring. It was a role Cohen intended for Joan Crawford.

Cohen didn't know Crawford, but since she had starred in a

With actor Michael Gough, Joan prepares for a scene in the circus.

host of horror films in recent years, including two for William Castle, he thought he had a good shot and convincing her into taking the role. "I wanted to try to pitch the lead to Joan Crawford, because I felt that Joan would be perfect for the picture," recalled Cohen. "Joan was a very close friend of Leo Jaffe, the president of Columbia Pictures at that time, and I asked Leo if he would introduce me to her. He was the one who made the introduction, and that's when I became friends with Joan Crawford."

Crawford was excited to have a starring role, even if it was a similar horror theme. But Cohen claimed she refused to look at the role that way. "With Joan and with Bette Davis, they never looked at these pictures as horror films - not even *Berserk!*," he said. "Joan just looked at it as a drama with some horrific moments."

But even so, Joan knew what she was getting into, but in convincing her Cohen knew focusing on the role and the story beyond the horror would sell her. "You had to be very careful - anyone who is a star never wants to feel they're going into a horror picture," he said. "You never use the word "horror" in front of them. In fact, the original title was "Circus of Blood" and she hated that title. Fortunately, we came up with the title *Berserk!*, which everybody loved."

Cohen also recalled that Crawford like the idea of going to the United Kingdom. "She was intrigued by the fact that *Berserk!* was going to be shot in London, because she loved London and the Brits loved her," he recalled. "And in England, she was still the Joan Crawford of yesteryear."

A Cut of the Proceeds

Crawford signed onto the film with her usual salary as well as a cut of the proceeds if the film did well. Having a stake in the success was a move that had paid off for many of her films in recent years. Even if the critics were unimpressed, if moviegoers came out to see her she was able to earn a good living off these films. For Cohen it also helped him keep her focused on getting the job done, having the film come in on time and under budget.

Crawford suggested they could keep the budget down by using some of her own clothes for her character to wear. "She also had me

Joan's main costume for the film was a black leotard designed by Edith Head as a personal favor to the star.

come to New York and pick out clothes from her own wardrobe what she should wear in these pictures - because she owned a big piece of both pictures, she didn't want us to spend any extra money on wardrobe," reported Cohen. "In her penthouse in New York she had a huge room, like a two-story room, with a ladder, and in it she kept all her clothes! And she knew where everything was, everything was catalogued!"

The one costume Crawford didn't have in her closet was an outfit suitable for her time in the ring. But she knew how to get one. She called in a favor from an old friend and asked Academy Award winning

Producer Herman Cohen entertained Crawford off the set.

costume designer Edith Head to design one for her. Head came through with a slimming black leotard, black stockings and a bright red coat with tails that took years off Crawford's age. Crawford also used the talent of make-up hairstylist Ramen Guy to take years off her age by designing "lifts" that pulled her skin back and lifted signs of sagging, hiding the tapes beneath her hairline. She was also carefully lit to hide her age.

Significant changes were made to the script to meet the star's requests and cast and crew arrived in London for filming. Cohen worked out the details for the shoot. "I made a deal with the Billy Smart Circus in England, to use their circus in the film. We shot at Shepperton Studios, then we also shot at night at the circus, after the place was closed, for about two weeks," he said.

Cohen vividly recalled working with Crawford on the film and doing what he could to please his star. "After she agreed to do the picture, of course we did a lot of changes on the script to make it fit her, and we had a lot of meetings prior to bringing her to London and shooting the picture. She was very much caught up in the idea of the story."

The producer felt that, "Knowing what kind of a big star she was, I did not want to diminish her stature in any way. Joan always thought of yesteryear, so I assigned her a Rolls-Royce with a chauffeur – even though it stretched the budget. I did whatever I could to make her realize that she was still Joan Crawford. She was revered in England. And we got great publicity there, not only from the tabloids but also *The London Times, The Sunday Times* and *The Observer*. Everybody did stories on her while we were shooting the picture."

The Story

In the film, Crawford stars as Monica Rivers, a woman who runs a traveling English circus she co-owns with a man named Dorando, played by Michael Gough. Monica acts as mistress of the ring while Dorando is the business manager, and the team is struggling to make ends meet and manage their band of circus misfits.

A horrifying death kicks off the film as Gaspar the Great in strangled and falls to his death after his tightrope has been sabotaged. Though his fans and coworkers are horrified, Monica considers that news of the tragedy will be good for business, so she hires a new high-wire act, played by Ty Hardin, and soon finds herself interested in more than his tightrope skills.

Monica begins to argue with Dorando over the best way to run the circus and he wants her to buy him out. She can't afford to and when Dorando is murdered a short time later Monica becomes the number one suspect.

More drama, mystery and mayhem ensue, including the murder of another circus member, played by Diana Dors who is killed by being sawed-in-half. As the movie reaches its climax, the new high-wire act is killed and it's discovered that Monica isn't the killer, but it's her daughter Angela, played by Judy Geeson. Angela has gone over the edge and wants to kill everyone who is stealing her mother's attention. She is

A lobby card to promote the star and the film.

139

electrocuted as she tries to escape during a lightening storm and Monica is left to go one with the show as the movie ends.

Director Jim O'Connolly fills out segments around the story with stock footage of the circus being constructed at stops along the way as well as the performing acts and the applauding crowds. The footage of animal acts and actual circus life offered an authenticity but kept production costs down.

Production

Cohen reportedly asked Crawford to lay off the liquor while shooting. Many who worked with Crawford in her later years knew she drank vodka from a frosted Pepsi-Cola glass. "She arrived with four cases of hundred-proof vodka, 'cause you can't get hundred-proof vodka in England," recalled Cohen. Even so, she reportedly told him she was "just a sipper," but respected his wishes and didn't drink while on set. She did manage to get the Pepsi name into the picture though and in one scene after one of the murders, a shot pans wide and viewers can see a Pepsi ad proclaiming "Come Alive! With Pepsi."

Cohen had a hard time escaping the star after the cameras shut down. He reportedly wined and dined her while in London and often received late calls from her at night. "She was taught everything at MGM, and one thing that she was taught there was that the producer is the boss," he said. "She always went to the producer if she had any problems, with the director or with any member of the cast or crew."

Cohen recalled, "… one morning she called me, about two o'clock a.m.—woke me up out of a sound sleep—asking, 'Herm, you have your script with you?' As if I go to bed with my script! She said, 'Go get your script! I'm working on tomorrow's scenes and you're sleeping!' I got the script, and she started in, 'Now, on page blah, blah, blah,' and she wanted to talk about it because, as I said, she was lonely. She would stay up late at night, sipping her vodka, going over her lines for the next day."

But the two struck up a friendship that lasted until her death, he said. "Joan was a very lonely lady, but we became very close friends, from the time of *Berserk!* until she died. We went out a lot, in London and New York and here in L.A., in the years after I met her on *Berserk!*

As for their time on the set he always found her professional and willing to put in the work necessary to get the job done. "In spite of her sipping hundred-proof vodka, she was very professional with me, and would never take a drink unless I okayed it," he recalled. "She always knew her lines and she was always on time."

Promotion of the film centered on the horror and less on the circus, although in some global markets the film was retitled 'Circus of Blood.'

He added that she would even arrive on the set early to make breakfast for the crew. "She would come in very early in the morning, like 6:30 a.m., and she loved to cook. She made breakfast for her hairdresser, for her costumer, for "her team. She was strong willed, she was tough - but, tough as she was, at the drop of a hat, she could be reduced to tears."

Cohen found Crawford to be quite caring of her fellow crew members. He even recalled during the shoot she called him late one evening to ask for a lift to the set even though he had arranged a car for her – a Rolls Royce at her disposal for the entire shoot.

"What time are you leaving for the studio tomorrow morning?" she reportedly asked him. "Look, why don't you leave around five-thirty and pick me up?"

Cohen asked, "Well, what's wrong with your car?"

"Oh, there's something wrong with the car," she said.

But there was nothing wrong with the car. Crawford has sent if off with one of film's prop men who had to have his teeth extracted. She supposedly sent her Rolls-Royce over to pick him up, take him to the dentist, wait for him, and take him home. She also sent it to a Jewish restaurant in Soho to pick up chicken soup and bring it to the prop man's house. "That's why she didn't have a car that day!" said Cohen. "So I had to call my driver, wake him up, and have him pick her up at five-thirty in the morning. She didn't tell me until after all this happened—in fact, it was the prop man who told me what Joan had done. But she was always doing this kind of stuff."

Columbia Pictures owned large apartment at the Grosvenor House on Park Lane in London at the time and for the production Cohen rented out the spacious location for Crawford's home away from home. It came with a support staff as well and Crawford got to know many of them during her stay. In fact, when she returned to London to film *Trog* for Cohen several years later the same apartment was rented for her again allowing he to return to familiar territory and she enjoyed seeing many of the same staff members the second time around.

It was also during this time that Joan's daughter Christina married director Harvey Medlinsky. And she gave her a big dinner party at Les Ambassadeurs, a popular London restaurant, to celebrate her new marriage. Cohen, who attended the event, recalled that Joan was happy for her daughter and saw no indication of trouble between the two. "Joan gave Christina a check for $5,000 and told her to enjoy herself. I was right there at the time. None of this is covered in *Mommie Dearest*," the book later was authored by Christina Crawford about her difficult relationship with her mother.

Reports from the set indicated that Crawford very much enjoyed making *Berserk!* In part because she was treated like a reigning movie star. The press in London adored her and the glamour of old Hollywood, as did many of the crew members on the production and her fellow actors. Also she was given very lavish treatment in her living accommodations at London's Grosvenor House, travelled to and from the set in a Rolls Royce, and had the full attention of her producer. When filming wrapped Crawford even gave a party for her fellow crew members.

Actress Judy Geeson, who played Crawford's troubled daughter in the film described her as "fabulous" adding that she "concentrates on her part with fantastic intensity and professionalism."

Crawford returned to New York after the shoot and the film was released months later in the fall of 1967. With tag lines like "Your front row seat to murder!" and "The motion picture that pits steel weapons against steel nerves!!!," the film first premiered in London in September 1967 and was a hit with the younger fans. In fact it was reportedly Columbia's second highest grossing film that year earning a reported $1.1 million. When it was released in the United States in early December it earned less attention and critics saw it mostly as just another continuation of the same horror slant Crawford, Davis and others had been on for much of the decade. Though all the reviews were not bad.

The *New York Times* reviewed the film by writing, "It's also hard to make a hopeless movie with a circus background and sawdust aroma. This is the one solid thing the picture has going for it—the intriguing workaday routine of circus folk and some good, spangly ring acts, all handsomely conveyed in excellent color photography. And under the reasonable direction of Jim O'Connolly, the film does project a kind of defiant suspense that dares you not to sit there, see who gets it next and, finally, why.

The Times also called Crawford "...professional as usual and certainly the shapeliest ringmaster ever to handle a ring microphone."

Lawrence Quirk reviewed the film for *Hollywood Screen Parade* writing, "[Crawford] is all over the picture, radiant, forceful, authoritative, a genuine movie star whose appeal never diminishes.

Other reviews offered similar, but unenthusiastic praise. *Variety* reviewed the film in December 1967, saying, "Story is full of holes, but it makes no difference ... an old fashioned thriller with more circus entertainment than plot or thrill, but it's got the name, the promotion, and the non-sophisticated audience appeal that makes this type of entertainment."

And *Time* reported in January 1968 that "Joan Crawford still has as pretty a set of gams as any actress in films. She displays them right up to the pelvis in the costume she wears as ring mistress and owner of an English circus, in which a killer at large perpetrates a parlay of improbable murders."

eleven

What Ever Happened to Mommie Dearest?

"If I weren't a Christian Scientist, and I saw 'Trog' (1970) adver-
tised on a marquee across the street, I'd think I'd contemplate
suicide."

- Joan Crawford

Crawford Tackles 'Trog'

As Roles Grow Slimmer the Star Settles for One Last Film

Joan Crawford learned the hard way. It's tough surviving in the movie business. Few actors have a lifetime of work, let alone success, and even fewer can be called survivors. Joan knew the struggle and she was a survivor.

Afrer six decades she had seen another decade go by. For

147

her the sixties had dawned with a renewed look at her life and career. Though she had lost her husband and very much needed to work, by 1962 she was on the verge of a full-fledged career resurgence. *What Ever Happened to Baby Jane?* gave her career a new lease on life. But it came with a price.

What followed were a series of scripts focusing on horror and less on strong performances. Acting was replaced by blood and gore. While her name was above the marquee she was playing second fiddle to killers, monsters and dead bodies. Her final film, *Trog* was the culmination of a career lasting 45 years and more than 80 films. But the film has

In 'Trog' Joan plays a scientist studying a pre-historic find.

been listed as her worst. Called "campy" and "deplorable," *Trog* goes down in history as one of her worst movies. It's been labeled a bomb in movie guides and TV listings and when it's shown on late-night TV viewers are often urged to stay away.

Yet something can draw fans to the screen. Crawford's youthful appeal had all but vanished by this point, but her fierce determination to survive kept her going. The film is worthy of viewing only for the fact that it marks her last screen appearance.

Trog was the final blow to a long an successful career. From an illustrious history as MGM's top box office draw and a string of smash hits, to her Oscar-winning performance in *Mildred Pierce*, Joan Crawford ended up playing second fiddle to an ancient caveman. It was sad end, as *Entertainment Weekly* wrote in a 1996 feature saying that the actress is mostly remembered as the villainess in *Mommie Dearest* and "has been relegated to the dubious pantheon of camp classics, the final resting place of so many tarnished Oscar victors."

Warner Bros. released the film in October 1970 and with poor reviews and a poor box office showing the film was banished to the late late show. Crawford herself refused to discuss it. She knew it was the end. It was one of the reasons she gave up performing. But her career was on the downhill by that point and there was little she could do about it. Crawford herself said in an interview with writer Roy Newquist "Now, please don't ask me about any pictures that followed *[What Ever Happened to] Baby Jane*. They were all terrible, even the few I thought might be good. I made them because I needed the money or because I was bored or both."

Even with the success of the *Baby Jane*, her career was in jeopardy. The film opened up a new genre for aging actresses. Horror films were cheap to make and solid box office draw. And they kept Crawford acting. But it was a downward spiral as the movies grew worse. Crawford saw practically nothing but horror films during the 60s. And as the decade drew to a close it was one last film to make before she gave up and began to move into retirement.

Another Cohen Horror

After the success of their last film together, *Berserk!*, Herman Cohen began thinking a follow-up picture would offer more of the same with, once again, Joan Crawford as the star. If he could come up with a script he had a feeling his star would be more than willing. The two got along well and struck up a friendship that continued after the filming ending and would go on for the remainder of Crawford's life.

Joan returned to England for her final feature film 'Trog.'

Before *Trog* Crawford was actually offered a supporting role in the film *Crooks and Coronets* which starred Telly Savalas, Warren Oates and Cesar Romero. The film was about a band of crooks hired to rob the estate of an eccentric old woman and Crawford was offered the role of the elderly woman. It's possible that the idea of playing an old woman on film was not the sort of role Crawford was after and she declined the offer, which went to Edith Evans. The film turned would earn excellent reviews and was far superior to *Trog*.

She also reportedly considered starring in two films for Italian producer-director Duccio Tessari. She also turned down a starring role in *The Bastard* reportedly over disagreements with the script and the film would end up with Rita Hayworth in the lead. Another proposed project, called "You'll Hang My Love" also never came together and the contract was never finalized and a final film, with or without Crawford, never resulted.

When Cohen approached Joan with a starring role in his next picture with the promise of a strong starring role and a cut of the proceeds she signed on. Originally titled "The Missing Link" the name was eventually changed to *Trog*, short for Troglodyte.

She had never had the lead in a film as a doctor or scientist, nor had she ventured into the world of science fiction so the film appealed to her. But the end result had more grounding in horror than science and would result in one of the lower-grossing and poorly reviewed films of her career.

The film was "a great experience," recalled Cohen years later. "*Trog* was based on an original story by Peter Bryan and John Gilling that I had bought, and then Aben [Kandel] and I wrote the screenplay. I changed the professor from a man to a woman; because we were so successful with *Berserk!* I wanted to do another picture with Joan."

Because *Berserk!* performed well at the box office the budget for

Trog was a bit more than the previous film, according to Cohen. Warner Bros. agreed to distribute the picture and it would be filmed at Bray Studios, the home of many Hammer horror pictures. Crawford would again head to the soundstages of London and additional exteriors would be shot

Joan used all her tricks to make herself look her best for the film.

in the English countryside. Key interior cave sequences would be shot on a set built at Bray.

"Fortunately, we got the same apartment for Joan that she had during *Berserk!* And Joan once again arrived at the spacious apartment at the Grosvenor House on Park Lane," said Cohen. "We rented it for Joan for *Trog*. Which was great, because she knew the whole staff—the maids, the waiters, everybody. It was like old home week. Joan also had a maid called Mamacita, who went with her wherever she went."

Joan once again offered to use her own wardrobe to allow the expenses to be spent elsewhere. Some stories suggest the budget didn't allow for a dressing room for Crawford in the English moors, but Cohen disputed this. "Untrue. She had a huge caravan—and I have reason to remember that well! We were out on location and it was quite chilly out, and I was told by my assistant that Joan was deathly ill in her caravan. I had my car take me there immediately, I went in to see her and she was saying [huffing and puffing], 'Oh, Herm.... oh!...get me a doctor...I can't work. I told her I'd do it, and I turned to run out. On these caravans, the door is low, and I ran and smashed my head against the top of the door [frame]—knocked myself for a loop! Joan jumped up and yelled, "Oh, Herman, Herman, darling! Come here, lie down!" She got a cold compress for my head—"You rest! I'll work!"— and within an hour, she was on the set! She forgot that she was sick, now that she was taking care of me!"

Star and Producer Aligned

Cohen enjoyed working with Joan so much so he invited his family to meet her. "During the making of *Trog*, I brought my three sisters over from the States, and Joan Crawford just took to them like they were her sisters. She gave a dinner party for them at Les Ambassadeurs, had a couple brunches, on and on. Joan was always 'The Movie Star'," he recalled.

But he also recalled how being a star made it hard for Crawford to enjoy herself. "There was many a Sunday when it was raining and cold in London, and a group of us from the film was going to go to a movie matinee. Joan said, 'I'd love to see that picture,' and I said, 'Come on!' She said, 'Oh, no, no, I'd have to get dressed.' 'No, you don't, just put a pair of slacks on.' And she said, 'I would never go out in a pair of slacks!'"

Joan was still working as a spokesperson for Pepsi, earning no more than $50,000 a year promoting the soft drink company, but it was not nearly enough to keep her living like Joan Crawford, said one biographer. And Crawford knew her days in the film business were numbered and she needed to plan for her future.

"People ask me why I took this science fiction role in *Trog*,"

Joan Crawford was disappointed with the final product when 'Trog' was released and decided to leave feature films behind. She did remain active with television work.

Crawford told one interviewer. "It's because I've never done any science fiction. I've never played a doctor before."

But the star was not entirely enthusiastic about the story and film and knew she was in the final stages of her working career. "I realized one morning that *Trog* was going to be my last picture. I had to be up early for the shoot and when I looked outside at the beautiful morning sky I felt that it was time to say goodbye. I think that may have been a prophetic thought because when I arrived on the set that morning the director told me that due to budget cuts we would wrap up filming today. The last shot of that film was a one-take and it was a very emotional moment for me. When I was walking up that hill towards the sunset I was flooded with memories of the last 50 years, and when the director yelled cut I just kept on walking. That for me was the perfect way to end my film career, however the audiences who had to sit through that picture may feel differently."

The Story of *Trog*

Originally titled "The Missing Link," the script would be another British-made film, directed by Freddie Francis and made on a low budget It would star Crawford as Dr. Brockton, a famous anthropologist who attempts to study an ape-like cave dweller that is half-man, half-ape, who is found by some young explorers in an underground cave. She names the beast *Trog* (short for Troglodyte) and tries to shape it by teaching it and treating it with kindness. "We're dealing with a backward child," says Dr. Brockton. "Surely we can teach him by example." But it appears to be, and as fate would have it, the creature is incapable of being civilized and escapes.

After a brief killing spree, Trog kidnaps a young girl and hides out in a cave. Crawford manages to get Trog to release the girl before authorities use gunfire and explosives to kill Trog, putting an end to the madness. Dr. Brockton, disillusioned, wanders away from the destruction as the credits role.

Trog isn't so much a horrific production as it is a bad film. Crawford was always professional on her film sets and *Trog* was no exception, even though the film's budget was minimal and the star herself earned only about $50,000 for the leading role. There are few details about the actual production but it appears the filming was performed on schedule with filming taking place in mid-1969 and wrapping up in August of the same year. On the set, actor David Warbeck played a reporter chasing the story and recalled in breaks between shooting Crawford giving him some words of advice. He said he was grateful for a few words she told him in the summer of 1969. "What we're paid for," she said, "is to turn shit into gold."

Crawford doesn't appear until 15 minutes into the film, but then appears in most every scene. She even manages to scale the caves, hard-hat, climbing equipment and all, to find Trog along with other explorers.

At the end she ventures into the caves once again, against the advice of authorities and with absolutely no equipment. She manages to single-handedly locate the beast and the girl, reason with Trog, convincing him to let her take the girl and then climb out of the cave with the girl in her arms. Authorities then charge into the caves, scaling its depths with extensive gear to reach the beast and then destroy it.

Trog's producer Cohen was called an "attractive, attentive and single" producer who treated his star as exactly that — a star. He took his star to dinner and the London theater, but no romance has ever been reported. Even so, Crawford became possessive. She would call him late at night to talk over the script and would demand to know where he was when he wasn't there to take her calls. The producer suspected she was lonely.

The star supplied her own clothes for wardrobe on her last few films, telling Cohen to save his money for other production costs. And when it came time to begin location shooting she arrived on the set in the gray English moors with 38 pieces of luggage. There were also rumors the star had a face-lift before the film. On *Berserk* she enjoyed the services of a gifted hairstylist named Ramen Guy who had performed his magic on another aging actress — Marlene Dietrich. Guy devised a series of six "lifts." These "lifts" were small tapes connected to rubber bands that came together behind the head and lifted and stretched the skin — erasing wrinkles and years. And while they may have also been used, it was also rumored that Crawford has some minor cosmetic surgery prior to filming to remove some wrinkles around her eyes.

She also had another beauty tip, which she once told to a woman's magazine writer. "There's a trick Claudette Colbert taught me years ago. Dump a tray of ice in your wash basin and splash ice water on your bazooms. It keeps them firm."

But beauty tips didn't erase the poor production and bad reviews that followed.

The Star's Drinking

It was fairly public knowledge that Crawford drank while working during her last years. Often it was disguised by her mixing vodka in a bottle of Pepsi Cola, but many knew. Crawford brought coolers of it to her movie sets and even managed to have it displayed on screen throughout several of her later films. Everyone knew she added something to her Pepsi. But even so, Crawford rarely had trouble remembering her lines or delaying production.

In some ways the film was reminiscent of *Frankenstein* with Trog as the beast and Crawford as the doctor who created/befriended it.

It wasn't just beauty tips that helped her get through filming. Crawford's drinking habits also helped her muster the strength to go on. … on *Trog*, her drinking was worse than it was when we were doing *Berserk!*," said Cohen. "I had to reprimand her a few times for drinking without asking. She had a huge frosted glass that said PEPSI-COLA— but inside was hundred-proof vodka! In fact, when she arrived to do *Berserk!* as well as *Trog*, she arrived with four cases of hundred-proof vodka, 'cause you can't get hundred-proof vodka in England. And when she arrived in both instances, she had something like forty pieces of luggage, and she had to arrange for Pepsi-Cola to send two trucks to meet the plane and pick it all up. These were huge cases, that she and Mamacita had packed themselves! And Joan knew where everything was, she was that organized. Now, I guarantee you that she didn't open seventy-five percent of these cases while she was in England, but obviously felt that she had to have 'em all there."

Cue Cards

But the drinking reportedly took its toll Crawford eventually had trouble remembering her lines. So, for some lengthy scenes her dialogue was printed on large printed cue cards for her to read. The cards were held up just outside the view of the camera and Crawford was able to get through some difficult scenes with lengthy dialogue, but Crawford was a bit embarrassed for needing them. "For the first time in my life I had to resort to using idiot boards," she admitted.

Director Freddie Francis confirmed that Crawford required cue cards. He claimed that by the time he made the film, Crawford had "gone past it." He said he was forced to use the cards and to keep he camera as immobile as possible so she could view the card as he filmed her. He also said that the footage from *The Animal World* was included only "to pad out the running time" because the shooting ran behind in the schedule.

A Forgettable Release

The film premiered in September 1970 with a broader release coming on October 24, 1970. To promote the film, Warner Bros. used the tag line, "FOUND: One missing link—and all the terror that goes with it!" Some promotion also used "Here comes *Trog*. You'll laugh at yourself for being so scared ...but don't laugh at *Trog*!

Crawford herself summed up *Trog* and her other flops by saying "At least a dozen of my bad pictures would have been good ones had they been given a decent script and a strong director."

In some markets the film was released as part of a double feature.

The Reviews Are In

Many critics wrote of their hopes that Crawford would escape
the horror film genre she had found herself forced into. The star herself
certainly would have. But she found work a challenge and once commented, "Frustrations are to work through, and even if you fail, the trying
enriches you."

The New York Times reviewed the film after its release in October 1970. Writer A.H. Weiler wrote *Trog* "proves that Joan Crawford is
grimly working at her craft. Unfortunately, the determined lady, who is
fetching in a variety of chic pant suits and dresses, has little else going
for her. ... *Trog* is no more exciting or scientific than the antics of a ram-
bunctious kid in a progressive school."

In the end, the film reportedly earned a little over $618,000 in
box office receipts and was billed mostly as part of a double feature,
released alongside Christopher Lee's *Dracula* horror. The film received
little notice and few film historians and Crawford biographers even
discuss the film in regards to Crawford's career. Some say that *Trog* had
"little significance" on the star's career and that it was only because of
the star's status that the movie wasn't tossed into the "B" movie category.

Variety reviewed the film in a September, 1970 issue suggesting that "*Trog* carries enough exploitable elements to score nicely in its
intended market where contrivance, a bit of corn and an imaginative
premise spell b.o. coin.... Freddie Francis's direction maintains a fast
and often suspenseful pace. ...Miss C is okay in her characterization,but
principal interest rests on the monster."

Crawford herself rated her 81st film as her worst, noting "If I
weren't a Christian Scientist, and I saw *Trog* advertised on a marquee
across the street, I'd think I'd contemplate suicide."

Dore Freeman, a longtime fan and collector of Crawford memorabilia, told the *New York Times* in 1977 that she all but vanished from public view. His autograph collection and correspondence with Crawford spanned 40 years. His last autograph from her came in October 1971, about a year after *Trog* was release. "During the last years she never liked to go out into public anymore," he said. "She was a movie star, a glamour queen. It would take so much time to prepare herself to be seen. Why do it? Nobody gave her any jobs."

Joan would continue to promote Pepsi until her retirement from the company in the early 1970s.

What Ever Happened to Mommie Dearest?

twelve

What Ever Happened to Mommie Dearest?

"Now you can understand why I retired from making motion pictures. Incidentally, I think at that point in my career I was doing my best work on television."

- Joan Crawford

The TV Years

Joan Crawford to the Small Screen Please

J oan had found television a viable source of income dating back practically to its inception. But it was really during the 50s when the movie roles grew more scarce that she obtained lucrative and frequent work on TV to supplement her income. When her movie career rebounded with *What Ever Happened to Baby Jane?* in 1962 she continued to accept work in television in part because the pay was good and the work was relatively easy.

She wasn't drawn to any specific type of work in TV, but in fact tried a lot of it. Talk shows from *The Tonight Show* to *Merv Griffin* and *The Mike Douglas Show* and others were easy enough and gave her a chance to promote a film, book, or her work with Pepsi-Cola and while there was an audience at times it was more about talking to the host conversationally and Joan excelled in the setting.

Another great way to play the part of a movie star, but in a brief and profitable way was in a game show. Usually no longer than a half-hour shows like *What's My Line, I've Got a Secret, Password* and others allowed her to be herself, but show a fun and interesting side her fans had not seen before.

One of Joan's most memorable television performances was in 'Night Gallery' in the early 1970s.

She also appeared in variety shows like *Hollywood Palace* and *The Bob Hope Show* and on awards shows like The Academy Awards and Emmy Awards broadcasts.

But aside from her appearances as herself she also tackled dramatic and comedy roles including *Della*, a TV movie in 1965 that was also briefly distributed as a feature film called *Fatal Confinement* and co-starred Diane Baker who Crawford had worked with several times before. Other dramatic appearances in *GE Theater* and the *Zane Grey Theater* in the 50s and 60s also offered her a chance to reach her fans in a new medium. In 1967 she had a cameo appearance in a special extended episode of *The Man From Uncle* and turned town an opportunity to appear in the highly popular *Batman* series.

Here's Joan

In 1968 she stepped into a movie star comedy role on *The Lucy Show* in an episode entitled "The Lost Star." It would be a chance to show her comedic side and Joan initially liked the idea. However, the experience didn't quite turn out that way.

Joan quickly found that working on the set of a short situation comedy like *The Lucy Show* required preparation and precision – crafts Lucille Ball had built into a fine-tuned art form. However, Joan was unaccustomed to the quick blocking and script rehearsals. She also feared performing in front of a live audience and reportedly took to more than a little drinking on the set. It made her rehearsals difficult when she couldn't remember her lines and follow key direction. Lucy was less than impressed with Crawford and at one point felt they should get rid of her and hire Gloria Swanson.

Crawford, in a panic, called her old friend Herman Cohen and told him, "They're trying to get rid of me."

Cohen told her to stick it out and not to leave and give them the chance. Joan pulled herself together and the show went off without a hitch and she surprised them all. "Joan, you were terrific," Ball reportedly told her afterwards. Ball then asked Crawford to go to dinner with her and her husband that evening.

Steven Spielberg directed Joan Crawford in one of his first Universal projects.

"Thank you, but I have an engagement," Crawford told her. That evening she invited members of the crew to go out to Don the Beachcomber's instead.

Working for Television

After the movie roles stopped coming some might have thought Joan Crawford had retired. But in reality, she wanted to work. One reason was financial, in that she wanted to ensure that in her real retirement years she would be able to support herself without fear of running out of money. She had heard many Hollywood of actors struggling to make ends meet in their sunset years. In fact her former husband Franchot Tone was one of them. Though she and Tone were only married from 1935 to 1939 they remained friends and many years later, as he struggled to care for himself and was confined to a wheelchair Crawford saw him often and helped him financially. She had him to her New York apartment and even vacationed with him in 1966 before cancer began to take its toll. In 1966 after he had a lung removed due to lung cancer he began to deteriorate. After he died in 1968 she saw to it his final wish was granted – that he be cremated and his ashes scattered over the Canadian woods near Muskoka.

In 1968, when her daughter Christina fell ill she entered the

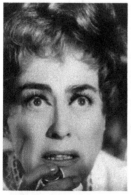

In an episode of 'The Sixth Sense,' which was also aired as part of 'The Night Gallery' series, Joan starred in an episode entitled "Deat Joan, We're Going to Scare You To Death."

hospital and was unable to make the set of the daytime soap opera *The Secret Storm*, in which she had a starring role. Joan contacted the producers and offered to stand in for her daughter until she recovered. Even though the character was supposed to be 25 and the two women held little resemblance it was not uncommon for actors to replace others on daytime soap operas. However, it was a bit shocking for some to see the older Crawford taking on the young role in a TV soap opera. But the casting provided a coup for the show and ratings went through the roof during the week she appeared. Some reports suggest she had a difficult time remembering her lines and required cue cards and used alcohol to calm her nerves making her at times drunk during the production.

Crawford's other reason for wanting to work was merely a desire to remain a star and continue to perform for her fans and public. Fortunately television presented her with several opportunities and she was able to work into the early 1970s.

The Night Gallery

Filmed and aired in 1969, *The Night Gallery* was a new series created by *Twilight Zone* creator Rod Serling. With each episode introduced by Serling, the shows centered on unusual, off-beat or odd coincidences that made up dramatic short features within the each episode. For the premiere episode three stories were to be told. One needed a strong leading lady.

Bette Davis was reportedly first approached with the role, but declined to appear. Crawford didn't hesitate. In fact, she became very involved in preparing for the part, but was bit concerned about the director.

Entitled "Eyes," the episode told the story of a rich older woman who is blind and spends her days in a penthouse apartment in Manhattan, but longs to see. She finds a man, played by Tom Bosley, willing to sell his eyes in order to pay off his gambling debts and buys them in order to gain her sight for the first time even though it is expected that her sight will only last for a number of hours. She blackmails a doctor, played by Barry Sullivan, into performing the operation and plans every last detail around what she wants to see and do as soon as the bandages are removed and she has her sight. Crawford co-starred with Sullivan in *Queen Bee.*

What she doesn't count on is a blackout. The story takes place during the 1965 blackout in New York City and as soon as her sight arrives all the lights go out and she spends the few hours she has with sight trapped in total darkness. Crawford spent weeks in her apartment walking around blindfolded in order to prepare for the part of a blind woman.

Directed by Steven Spielberg, who was recently hired to Universal for his first directorial efforts, Crawford was a bit taken back with his youth and concerned. "He couldn't possibly have enough experience," she reportedly said. "How could I feel reassured the way an experienced director is supposed to make you feel?"

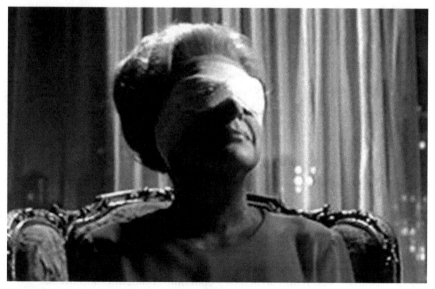

Joan portrayed a blind woman who purchases eyes in order to see in one of her last television projects.

"Wait'll you meet him," the producer responded. And when she did, she thought he looked like he was "about 12 years old" instead of 22 at the time. But Crawford's hesitation gradually disappeared after she began working with the young director. The show would be one of the highlights of the series and would kick off a successful three season run.

When she met him she was reportedly blindfolded and preparing for the role and didn't initially see him, but rather heard him. She had called him with concerns about dialogue and suggested they meet in person and he arrived to find her with her eyes covered and practicing to be blind. "I never got over the idea of directing Joan Crawford," Spielberg once recalled. "It was a quantum leap."

Over dinner she offered him some advice he held onto. "Now, I know what television schedules are like, and I know the pressure that will be on you to finish the show on time. You'll want your first work as a director to be something you can be proud of, and I'll break my ass to help you. Don't let any executive bug you because the picture's not on schedule. If you have any problems with the Black Tower, let me take care of it. I'll be your guardian angel. Okay?" [The Black Tower, was a common nickname for the executive offices of Universal where the executive staff called the shots.]

Spielberg said of the experience, "Directing Joan Crawford was like pitching to Hank Aaron your first time in the game." He studied her films before working with her and summed her up by saying, "She is five-feet-four, but she looks six-feet on the screen. In a two-shot with anyone, even Gable, your eyes fix on her. She is imperious, yet with a childlike sparkle. She is haughty, yet tender. She has no great range as an actress, yet within the range she can perform better than any of her contemporaries."

She arrived with cartons of Pepsi and vodka and had the set temperature brought down to her usual 55 degrees. But other than that he found the experience a pleasure. He said Crawford "treated me like I had been directing for 50 years. She was very good to me, very firm, but very kind. I called her Miss Crawford and she insisted on calling me Mr. Spielberg. I asked her to call me Steven, but she wouldn't. She knew I was a scared kid, and she was setting an example – of courtesy, and yes, of respect – for the rest of the cast and crew to follow."

He believed that once she found confidence in him as a director he gained her respect. "Once she knew I had done my homework – I had my storyboards right there with me every minute – she treated me as if I was The Director."

He did cater to her needs. In addition to the cold set he provided her with cue cards to help her with her lines during shooting after she began to have trouble with the dialogue. Tom Bosley recalled that one of the reasons she had trouble with her lines was her drinking. "It was one of the strangest shooting experiences I've ever been involved in," he said. "I don't know how else to put it, except to say that I think she was dead drunk most of the time."

Bosley said the trouble was hardest on Spielberg. "We spent a lot of time watching Steven shoot around Miss Crawford. I just felt terribly sorry for him."

But Crawford did eventually arrive on set and managed to get through her scenes. Some saw her behavior and fear more than ego. And as she aged she knew the camera would capture that and the fear of being surrounded by so many new actors and crew members, as well as different shooting schedules and technology changes only illustrated how much her business was changing. And that brought about her fear.

The episode was eventually completed and aired on a Sunday evening, November 8, 1969, earning strong enough ratings to get the series picked up by NBC for a full season. Serling would even go on to earn an Emmy Award for his work on the series that year. The show-would lead to another project after she completed her work on *Trog*.

The Sixth Sense

In 1972 Crawford was offered a chance to star in a dramatic series called *The Sixth Sense*. A weekly mystery-suspense series similar to *The Night Gallery* and *Twilight Zone*, the series delved into ESP, psychic phenomenon and otherworldly adventures. Her episode, entitled "Dear Joan, We're Going to Scare You To Death" centered on her supposedly being driven crazy or frightened to death. In the show Crawford plays Joan Fairchild, a woman who with car trouble who runs off the road. She begins having visions of a young woman drowning in a lake. With her car out of commission she seeks help at a nearby home inhabited by a group of young people experimenting with the occult and ESP. The kids invite her in for the night until she can get her car fixed in the morning. Unbeknownst to her, they attempt to use their psychic abilities to telepathically terrorize her with images of her deceased daughter. But their attempts to frighten her to death fail and her visions of a young woman drowning become reality with Joan coming to the aid of the young woman.

Even though it was only a guest appearance on a TV show, Crawford was flown into Hollywood and treated like royalty. She was put up in a Hollywood bungalow and had visits from Rock Hudson, Alfred Hitchcock and Lew Wasserman, head of Universal. She also had her maid, Mamacita, and her dog along with her and was driven to the set in a limousine. She even managed to get the cameraman of her choice hired for the series, telling the producers "Look, I'm no longer an ingénue. I need someone who knows how to light me."

The filming lasted seven days and Crawford reportedly impressed everyone in attendance with her professionalism and performance. When she arrived they apparently saw her as "small and fragile, a woman on the brink of old age." However, once she transformed herself into the Joan Crawford for the screen the legendary star emerged. After filming her final scene the cast and crew erupted in applause and a cast party was held after the show wrapped. One report said that even though Joan was "slightly drunk" as the festivities progressed she was able to remember the names of everyone in the crew and they each received thank you letters afterwards.

Crawford would ultimately find some of her television work far more rewarding than that of her last feature films.

When discussing her last decade of work with one interviewer she explained, "I hate being asked to discuss those dreadful horror pictures I made the mistake of starring in. They were all just so disappointing to me, I really had high expectations for some of them. I thought that William Castle and I did our best on *Strait-Jacket* but the script was ludicrous and unbelievable and that destroyed that picture. I even thought that *Berserk!* would be good but that was one of the worst of the lot. The other one William Castle and I did was the most wretched of them all and I just wasn`t good at playing an over-the-hill nymphomaniac. Ha! Then came *Trog*. Now you can understand why I retired from making motion pictures. Incidentally, I think at that point in my career I was doing my best work on television. *Della* was a good television role for me, and I really liked working on that pilot episode of *Night Gallery* with young Steven Spielberg. He did a great job and I am very satisfied with my performance on that show. Funny, every time a reporter asks me about my horror pictures they never talk about that one, and it's the only one I liked!"

What Ever Happened to Mommie Dearest?

thirteen

What Ever Happened to Mommie Dearest?

I hate being asked to discuss those dreadful horror pictures I made the mistake of starring in. They were all just so disappointing to me, I really had high expectations for some of them.

- Joan Crawford

The Later Years

The Movie Star Begins Downsizing her World and Receding from Public Life

s Joan Crawford receded from the world of a celebrated movie star she became more and more reclusive and reluctant to go out. In large part because she felt it took too much energy to turn herself into the glamorous movie star she felt her fans expected and deserved.

179

But in the spring of 1974 she had another reason to fear going out.

She received a phone call from an anonymous caller that was recorded on her answering machine. The caller threatened her, "to kidnap her, or worse" if she were to step outside.

Crawford had her share of haters in her life. Bad reviews, unkind directors – and the trauma of sharing the soundstage with Bette Davis – had been difficult to endure, but never had she felt afraid for her life from an anonymous someone who might be waiting just outside her door.

The police were called and the FBI was brought in. Crawford's apartment was put under surveillance for almost a month and several "suspects" were even brought in for questioning, however no charges were ever filed against anyone and they never figured out who had threatened her.

Joan decided to beef up her security and installed an alarm system in her apartment. And the doorman who secured the lobby of her apartment complex had instructions to identify and obtain permission before sending guests up to her home. She even got into the habit of answering the phone in a disguised voice, acting as her own maid, so callers wouldn't know it was her.

She had a few friends and fans who visited her and enjoyed visits from her twin daughters who were now grown with children and lives of their own. She seldom saw Christina, her eldest daughter and refused to see her son Christopher. She claimed she had tried to get through to him years earlier, but his hatred of her drove her to give up on him. " I remember most clearly," she recalled. "When a teenage Christopher spat in my face. He said 'I hate you.' It's pretty hard to overlook that. I couldn't."

She once said she had adopted her two oldest children, "but they didn't adopt her."

Christopher reportedly did try to reach out to his mother after returning from a stint in Vietnam during the war, but he was turned away by the doorman. It is unclear whether Joan refused his visit or wasn't aware it was actually her son. However, a reconciliation between the two never occurred and she never did see her son again.

Town Hall and One Last Part

In 1973 she was invited to appear on stage for and appearance in "Legendary Ladies at Town Hall." Publicist and writer John Springer had arranged a series of events featuring iconic leading ladies including Bette Davis, Myrna Loy and others and when Ginger Rogers agreed to appear and then abruptly cancelled, Springer approached Crawford to take her place. Crawford was fearful of crowds and live appearances so he never expected her to accept, but it would mark one of the most memorable moments of the series as Crawford took questions and spoke candidly about her life and career. She received massive applause and a standing ovation. As flowers were tossed onto the stage at the end of the show she grew emotional, but stayed long enough to pick up and accept each flower tossed to her. The crowd adored her.

After the success of the appearance several offers came her way. One was a revised version of the stage play *Sleuth*, that was intended to be staged with her in one of the leads, but she turned it down fearing she would never be up to the pace of live theater.

Then in 1974 there was an effort to translate the Broadway hit *Follies* into a film. The film would change the story from the theater to Hollywood's golden age and the fall of the studio system. A broad collection of Hollywood stars were rumored to be set with starring roles. Elizabeth Taylor, Henry Fonda, Bette Davis, Gene Kelly, Shirley MacLaine, Janet Leigh and Debbie Reynolds were named to the cast – along with

Joan Crawford.

Crawford was to play a version of the stage role that earned acclaim for Yvonne DeCarlo. It would be the role of a former dancer, not unlike Crawford's early years in the business. But the film would fall apart when MGM had disagreements with the producer of the show. Some stories suggest that money became one of the factors and the cost of all the stars was going to make the budget for the film skyrocket. In the end the film never came to pass and Crawford was disappointed at not having a chance to film one last good feature.

Joan Crawford took to the stage for a special event. Though she always feared a live audience she was touched by the applause of her fans at one of her final public appearances.

One Last Outing

Also in 1974 writer John Springer authored a book called *They Had Faces Then*. A look back at the glamorous leading ladies of Hollywood's golden era, the book was published by Citadel Press and Joan was thrilled to learn that a man she had grown very fond of was celebrating a topic she held dear.

Crawford offered to hold a party upon the release of the book and Springer accepted. As the event was being planned Springer reportedly began to get cold feet. He was more used to being on the side of the interviewer and the host rather than the celebrity or object of all the attention.

Springer remembered that Rosalind Russell was still in New York from an appearance in "Legendary Ladies," his series of Town Hall interviews that had celebrated numerous leading ladies including Joan Crawford. Since Crawford and Russell were old friends, but seldom saw each other because Crawford remained in New York while Russell lived in Los Angeles, he thought it might be nice to bring the two together. Springer suggested having Russell cohost the event and celebrate the evening as a bringing together of two legendary leading ladies as much as it was the launch of his book about the same topic. Crawford agreed and Russell took part in the event as well.

Dressed in her best gown and draped in jewels Joan did her best to become the Joan Crawford everyone knew and loved. Russell did the same but injections of cortisone for painful rheumatoid arthritis left her face looking bloated. Everyone appeared to have a great evening and those in attendance said Crawford "looked stunning."

The press, however, was on hand for the event and pictures promoting the event found their way into newspapers across the country the next day. The pictures chosen were far from becoming and Crawford was horrified by the way she and Russell appeared. "If that's the way I look," she remarked after seeing the pictures. "No one's going to see me any more."

The End of Pepsi

Crawford also ended her association with Pepsi about the same time as the event. She was forced into retirement by PepsiCo around 1973, but she continued to earn a pension and promote the soft drink when asked. When she turned 65, which according to her PR machine was in 1973 (she was actually closer to 69), the company forced her to officially retire.

Joan in her home during her years in retirement. She spent much of her time surrounded by her pets.

When she was invited to be the guest of honor at Pepsi's convention in San Francisco in 1974 she declined. After seeing herself in the press she decided it was time to hang up her promotional days as well. She also didn't like the new top executive at Pepsi, Don Kendall, who she referred to as "Fang" after Phyllis Diller's fictional husband from her comedy act.

But Crawford remained tied to PepsiCo no matter what, much to the chagrin of Kendall. In fact Kendall was known to be introduced at parties as "the man with Joan Crawford's company," and for many years he would receive mail at the New York headquarters addressed to "Joan Crawford, President of Pepsi-Cola."

Downsizing

On the home-front Crawford also had begun downsizing. In 1972 when her building, The Imperial House, went condo she bought a smaller apartment in the building for $100,000 and moved out of her larger unit shedding many of the Hollywood mementos and remnants of her past life as a movie star. Those who visited her home, apartment 22G at 150 East 69th Street in New York, during the last years of her life said one would never know a movie star like Joan Crawford lived there. No photos and trappings of her Hollywood years remained. She also reportedly gave up her driver and limousine service. Though she retained the help of Mamacita, her longtime cook, housekeeper and friend, as well as help from an part-time houseman who helped with heavy lifting and cleaning. And her loyal secretary Betty Barker remained with her to the end.

She had few guests, but occasionally entertained and dined at home with friends and longtime fans that she had kept in touch with. Crawford also remained heavily focused on her correspondence and was very much known for her frequent and regular cards and letters. She responded to nearly every fan letter or contact from a friend and it was the one true thing that remained of her years as a Hollywood glamour queen.

The Last of the Movie Offers

While she had for the most part retired, Crawford still entertained the idea that there might be once last movie role for her. And occasionally she got an interesting offer. She was offered a part in *Airport '77* and *Superman*, among others, but ultimately would decline the chance to reconnect with her fans on the big screen.

fourteen

What Ever Happened to Mommie Dearest?

Send me flowers while I'm alive. They won't do me a damn bit of good after I'm dead."

- Joan Crawford

The End of a Movie Star

Joan Crawford Succumbs to Cancer on May 10, 1977

I n September 1976 Joan Crawford gave her last "public" performance when she left her home for her final photo shoot. It was to be included with her Christmas card that year and Crawford appeared with her dog, a shih-tzu she had named Princess Lotus Blossom. Fully made up Crawford she appeared with her natural fine pale gray, styled up and back. While she had lost weight and appeared much thinner than many remembered her, her wide expressive eyes were still the same.

Photographer John Engstead, snapped the last images of the star. He had photographed her many years earlier when she was making *Mildred Pierce*, and the final photos captured the essence of Joan Crawford, with the glamour and beauty she wanted the world to see, but also showed the passage of time.

With the dawn of 1977 she had resigned herself to the fact that her movie career had ended and there would be no more film roles. Her last offer of work came the previous year when she was offered a role in the film *Airport '77*. It would have been the role of Emily Livingston, a rich and elegant socialite who loved to gamble. But Crawford reportedly felt the film schedule was too compressed and she wouldn't have enough time to prepare for the role. She declined the offer though she would very much loved to have had one last role to be remembered by. She would have had the chance to play opposite Joseph Cotton. The two had last worked on the same set in *Hush, Hush ... Sweet Charlotte*, though Crawford exited the film before completing it. And history repeated itself when Olivia De Havilland was offered and accepted the part to replace Crawford as she had done nearly 15 years earlier.

A Fight Against Time

In the final year of her life she was reportedly diagnosed with pancreatic cancer, but her belief in the teachings of Christian Science left her unwilling to fight the disease. The Church's teachings suggest that God is good and illness, like evil, is not real. It implies that medical treatment is not necessary to overcome ills. The teachings also said drinking and smoking were evils one should avoid. Joan had ignored those passages for many years, but it was reported that after suffering a nasty fall while alone in her later years after having a bit too much to drink one evening convinced her it was time to give up alcohol.

Joan was determined to die at home. She told friends she wanted to die in the comfort of her own bedroom and during her final months she became a recluse, living out her last days at home watching old movies and remembering the many friends and lovers who she had already lost like Alfred Steele, Clark Gable, Franchot Tone, John Garfield, William Haines and many others. "I don't know when I will die, or of what I will die," she said. "But I do know where I will die – at home, in my bedroom. I don't have control over the other two factors. But I do have control over where, unless I have an accident. Otherwise it will be in my own bed, in my own home."

She had learned in the last year of her life also that her daughter Christina was writing a book about her. She knew the tale would not be

While still looking every bit a movie star Joan Crawford's professional photos showed off her gray hair. She would use the shots when responding to fan letters in her later years.

a kind one, suggesting that had it been she would have told her herself about the book and asked for her help.

"I think she's using my name strictly to make money," Joan reportedly commented to writer John Springer when he asked her if she was aware of her daughter's book. "I suppose she doesn't think I am going to leave her enough, or that I'm going to disappear soon enough."

Asked whether she wanted to know what it was about, she said, "I plan not to read it. Why spoil days of your life reading a book that can only hurt you. Once you've read it, the words stay with you and torture you. The book produces a bad aura, which costs days of your life."

She went on to tell Springer, "I think this book will be full of lies and twisted truths."

The End

She had told no one she was ill – no close friends, not even her children. By the end of April she was reportedly down to less than 100 pounds and the cancer had made it difficult for her to even get around her own home. She spent Mother's Day bedridden and on May 9 she decided she was no longer able to care for her beloved dog, Princess Lotus Blossom, so she found a suitable home in the country for her and gave her away to friends.

On the morning of May 10, 1977 she rose early in the day and got up, dressed in a gown and robe and went to the kitchen to cook breakfast. While she herself had no appetite and not much strength, her housekeeper and a long-time fan were there and were part of a very small group who knew Joan was ill. They spent the night in her apartment, watching an old movie with her and looking after her to keep her company in case she needed anything. The date also marked what would have been her 22nd wedding anniversary to Alfred Steele. She wanted to repay their kindness by fixing them breakfast.

Her breakfast of tea and graham crackers was brought in to her about 10 a.m. but before she could have any she passed away. One story suggests that her housekeeper attended to her in her final hours and began to pray for her as she lay dying. The story goes that Joan Crawford looked at her housekeeper and said, "Damn it...Don't you dare ask God to help me."

Headline News

The news of her death made front-page headlines across the country and around the world. She asked that the cause of death be listed as a heart attack rather than cancer. She was called "the quintessential superstar." Joan had listed out all the instructions for her final wishes after her death.

She was to be cremated and placed in an urn that was to be put alongside her late husband, Alfred Steele, at Ferncliff Cemetery in Westchester County, New York. A service was held in New York City at Campbell's Funeral Home on May 13,1977. Myrna Loy, Van Johnson, John Springer and three of Joan's four children (Cathy, Christina and Christopher), along with many others, were in attendance. Another service, reportedly arranged by PepsiCo for her longtime work there, was held in on May 17 at the All Souls Unitarian Church on Lexington Avenue in New York with George Cukor, Anita Loos, Pearl Bailey, Cliff Robertson and other Hollywood friends paying their last respects. Christina and Cindy Crawford also attended. Bailey called Crawford her sister and sang a favorite hymn, "He'll Understand." Another service was held in Beverly Hills.

Much has been written about her last will and testament, the final bequeaths made and not made. It was made in October 1976, little

193

more than six months before her actual death. She left an estate valued at about $2 million. And while a large portion was left to charities she held dear, she provided $77,500 each to her adopted twin daughters Cathy and Cynthia and $5,000 to each of their children, as well as $35,000 to her loyal secretary and friend Betty Barker. And aside from some small gifts, the remained was divided up between The USO of Metropolitan New York, where she was once a director and vice president; the Motion Picture Home and Hospital, which she faithfully funded for many years of her life; the Muscular Dystrophy Association, where she was a corporate member; and several other charities like The American Cancer Society, the American Heart Association, an the Wiltwyck School for Boys.

Her final remarks were, "It is my intention to make no provision herein for my son Christopher or my daughter Christina for reasons which are well known to them." It wasn't a surprise to many who knew her, though the press ate it up as a juicy story of a troubled family. Carl Johnes, a friend of Crawford's said she once told him, "Tina and Christopher are just waiting for me to die. That's all they want."

And when Johnes replied, "But surely there's something you can

Joan downsized her apartment living to a smaller place in later years.

do about that," hinting at a reconciliation beginning with her.

She deadpanned, "Yes, there is. I can cut them out of my will!" And so she did.

Christina and Christopher reportedly contested the will, claiming their mother was incompetent when the will was signed. They received a settlement of $55,000 to split between them.

For Christina, her book would be her inheritance and the money she earned from it could be considered earnings off the image of Joan Crawford – the one she tried to destroy. For Christopher, he had cut her off as much as she him. There was no love lost there on either side, some suggest, and in many ways he had grown up a stranger to her.

After her death, Jack Valenti, president of the Motion Picture Association of America at the time, asked all of the major Hollywood studios to observe a moment of silence in her honor. It's something that has rarely been done, but all the studios agreed. Crawford has worked for most of them at one time or another under contract or as an independent actor. "Joan Crawford deserved the honor as an icon," he said. "It was a professional honor, paying tribute to her career and what it had meant all those years in Hollywood."

As cancer took its toll Joan Crawford spent her last days in the bedroom of her New York apartment. She saw few visitors.

What Ever Happened to Mommie Dearest?

fifteen

What Ever Happened to Mommie Dearest?

"If you're going to be a star, you have to look like a star, and I never go out unless I look like Joan Crawford the movie star."

- Joan Crawford

Closing Remarks

What Remains of the Legend Today

George Cukor once said of her, "The camera saw a side of her that no flesh and blood lover ever saw." And while some may have felt that comment could be a double-edged sword, for Joan Crawford it may perhaps be the ultimate compliment. For, in reality, Joan Crawford was a cinema creation that evolved, over the years, into a living, breathing person.

199

Born under another name, into humble beginnings and less-than-fortunate surroundings, her early life was no picnic. Her relationship with her mother was tenuous at best and she endured a love-hate relationship with her brother that held little love. A father she never really knew left her longing for a strong man in her life. It was a desire she carried with her through much of her adult life. In fact, her desire for family, in general, was spun out of a childhood that lacked the Norman Rockwell image so many of us strive for, but few of us have.

Not long after she reached Hollywood she was rechristened Joan Crawford and shed the old Lucille Fay LeSueur persona, putting her into a box she hid deep away in her closet. She never forgot who she was or where she'd come from. In fact, some might say she held deep respect for her past. It showed her what her life could have been, had she not struggled, fought and drove herself to achieve what few ever would – to become the be the number one box office movie star in the world.

But surviving in Hollywood gets tougher the longer you go on. And by the 1950s she was considered old news. She, again, refused to accept what others would tell her and struggled to make it on her own. She acquired independent film productions and negotiated her own picture deals at major studios and managed to prove them wrong again and again.

At the same time she longed for family. She knew her career would not keep her warm at night or be there to comfort her in her old age. A strong husband and adoring children were part of her plan, but that, in some ways was a harder image and persona to achieve. Marriages ended unhappily and, at best, she got a 50 percent success rate with her children. Two remained by her side until the end, another hated her and a fourth – her first – would battle with her to the end and even beyond, publishing a book that nearly destroyed the image she spent 50 years building.

Joan Crawford was the creation of some publicity men in Hollywood, but by the time it was all over she was flesh and blood. And she loved the name, saying at one point she was Joan Crawford and the name had stuck with her becoming that creation and that creation becoming her. And in the years since the release of *Mommie Dearest*, that image goes on. In fact, in some ways she has recovered from that tell-all tale to reclaim her spot in movie-stardom. No, she may never truly escape the tales spun by her daughter. Only those present know the real story. But as

Joan was buried next to her last husband, Alfred Steele after her death in May 1977.

a movie star, an actress, and an entertainer, her legend lives on. So much so that The American Film Institute named her the tenth greatest female star in the history of American cinema.

Those who knew her say the real individual was shy and reluctant to talk about herself. She was afraid of live audiences and large gatherings and didn't enjoy talking about her personal life. But when she got in front of a camera something happened and the persona truly came to life. Even in the later years, when the films failed to deliver the Academy Award nominations and the budgets and scripts were less than what she might have hoped for. Still, when the camera came on she gave it her 100 percent and regardless of whether it was *Grand Hotel* or the Grand Guignol of *What Ever Happened to Baby Jane?*, it was still Joan Crawford right down to the last shot. And it still is.

appendix

What Ever Happened to Mommie Dearest?

filmography

What Ever Happened to Mommie Dearest?

"I was born in front of a camera and really don't know anything else."

- Joan Crawford

Filmography

The Work of Joan Crawford

Feature Films

Lady of the Night (1925) (MGM) (uncredited) ... Norma Shearer double

Proud Flesh (1925) (MGM) (uncredited) ... bit part

A Slave of Fashion (1925) (MGM) (uncredited) ... mannequin

The Merry Widow (1925) (MGM) (uncredited) ... extra

Pretty Ladies (1925) (MGM) (credited as Lucille LeSueur) ... Bobby

The Circle (1925) (MGM) (uncredited) ... Young Lady Catherine

The Midshipman (1925) (MGM) (uncredited) ... extra

Old Clothes (1925) (MGM) (credited as Lucille LeSueur) ... Mary Riley

The Only Thing (1925) (MGM) (uncredited) ... party guest

Sally, Irene and Mary (1925) (MGM) (credited as Joan Crawford) ... Irene

Tramp, Tramp, Tramp (1926) (FIRST NATIONAL) ... Betty Burton

Paris (1926) (MGM) ... the girl

The Boob (1926) (MGM) ... Jane

Winners of the Wilderness (1927) (MGM) ... Ren'e Contrecoeur

The Taxi Dancer (1927) (MGM) ... Joslyn Poe

The Understanding Heart (1927) (MGM) ... Monica Dale

The Unknown (1927) (MGM) ... Estellita or Nanon, Zanzi's Daughter

Twelve Miles Out (1927) (MGM) ... Jane

Spring Fever (1927) (MGM) ... Allie Monte

Dream of Love (1928) (MGM) ... Adrienne Lecouvreur

Our Dancing Daughters (1928) (Cosmopolitan Production/MGM) ... Diana Medford

Four Walls (1928) (MGM) ... Frieda

Across to Singapore (1928) (MGM) ... Priscilla Crowninshield

Rose-Marie (1928) (MGM) ... Rose-Marie

The Law of the Range (1928) (MGM) ... Betty Dallas

West Point (1928) (MGM) ... Betty Channing

Hollywood Snapshots #11 (1929) (MGM) ... Herself

The Hollywood Revue of 1929 (1929) (MGM) ... Herself

Untamed (1929) (MGM) ... Alice "Bingo" Dowling

Our Modern Maidens (1929) (MGM) ... Billie Brown

The Duke Steps Out (1929) (MGM) ... Susie

Paid (1930) (MGM) ... Mary Turner

Our Blushing Brides (1930) (MGM) ... Gerry Marsh

Montana Moon (1930) (MGM) ... Joan "Montana" Prescott

Possessed (1931) (MGM) ... Marian Martin

This Modern Age (1931) (MGM) ... Valentine "Val" Winters

Laughing Sinners (1931) (MGM) ... Ivy "Bunny" Stevens

The Slippery Pearls (1931) ... Herself

Dance, Fools, Dance (1931) (MGM) ... Bonnie "Bon" Jordan

Letty Lynton (1932) (MGM) ... Letty Lynton

Grand Hotel (1932) (MGM) ... Flaemmchen

Rain (1932) (UNITED ARTISTS) ... Sadie Thompson

Screen Snapshots (1932) ... Herself

Today We Live (1933) (MGM) ... Diana "Ann" Boyce-Smith

Dancing Lady (1933) (MGM) ... Janie "Duchess" Barlow

Sadie McKee (1934) (MGM) ... Sadie McKee Brennan

Chained (1934) (MGM) ... Diane Lovering, also called "Dinah"

Forsaking All Others (1934) (MGM) ... Mary Clay

No More Ladies (1935) (MGM) ... Marcia Townsend

I Live My Life (1935) (MGM) ... Kay Bentley

The Gorgeous Hussy (1936) (MGM) ... Margaret O'Neal "Peggy" Eaton

Love on the Run (1936) (MGM) ... Sally Parker

The Bride Wore Red (1937) (MGM) ... Anni Pavlovitch

The Last of Mrs. Cheyney (1937) (MGM) ... Fay Cheyney

Mannequin (1937) (MGM) ... Jessica Cassidy

The Shining Hour (1938) (MGM) ... Olivia Riley

Ice Follies of 1939 (1939) (MGM) ... Mary McKay

The Women (1939) (MGM) ... Crystal Allen

Strange Cargo (1940) (MGM) ... Julie

Susan and God (1940) (MGM) ... Susan Trexel

A Woman's Face (1941) (MGM) ... Anna Holm

When Ladies Meet (1941) (MGM) ... Mary Howard

They All Kissed the Bride (1942) (COLUMBIA) ... Margaret Drew

Reunion in France (1942) (MGM) ... Michelle de la Becque

Above Suspicion (1943) (MGM) ... Frances Myles

Hollywood Canteen (1944) (WARNER BROS.) ... Herself

Mildred Pierce (1945) (WARNER BROS.) ... Mildred Pierce

Humoresque (1946) (WARNER BROS.) ... Helen Wright

Possessed (1947) (WARNER BROS.) ... Louise Howell Graham

Daisy Kenyon (1947) (20TH CENTURY FOX) ... Daisy Kenyon

Flamingo Road (1949) (WARNER BROS.) ... Lane Bellamy

It's a Great Feeling (1949) (WARNER BROS.) (uncredited) ... Herself

The Damned Don't Cry (1950) (WARNER BROS.) ... Ethel Whitehead/
Lorna Hansen Forbes

Harriet Craig (1950) (COLUMBIA) ... Harriet Craig

Goodbye, My Fancy (1951) (WARNER BROS.) ... Agatha Reed

This Woman Is Dangerous (1952) (WARNER BROS.) ... Beth Austin

Sudden Fear (1952) (RKO) ... Myra Hudson

Torch Song (1953) (MGM) ... Jenny Stewart

Johnny Guitar (1954) (REPUBLIC) ... Vienna

Female on the Beach (1955) (UNIVERSAL) ... Lynn Markham

Queen Bee (1955) (COLUMBIA) ... Eva Phillips

Autumn Leaves (1956) (COLUMBIA) ... Millicent Wetherby

The Story of Esther Costello (1957) (VALIANT FILMS/COLUMBIA) ...
Margaret Landi

The Best of Everything (1959) (20TH CENTURY FOX) ... Amanda
Farrow

What Ever Happened to Baby Jane (1962) (SEVEN ARTS/WARNER
BROS.) ... Blanche Hudson

The Caretakers (1963) (UNITED ARTISTS) ... Lucretia Terry

Strait-Jacket (1964) (COLUMBIA) ... Lucy Harbin

I Saw What You Did (1965) (UNIVERSAL) ... Amy Nelson

Berserk! (1968) (COLUMBIA) ... Monica Rivers

Trog (1970) (WARNER BROS.) ... Dr. Brockton

Television Performances

Revlon's Mirror Theater (1953) (CBS) "Because I Love Him" ... Margaret Hughes

General Electric Theater (1954) (CBS) "The Road to Edinburgh" ... Mary Andrews

General Electric Theater (1958) (CBS) "Strange Witness" ... Ruth

General Electric Theater (1959) (CBS) "And One Was Loyal" ... Ann Howard

The Joan Crawford Show (1959) (Pilot) "Woman On The Run" ... Susan Conrad

Dick Powell's Zane Grey Theater (1959) (CBS) "Rebel Range" ... Stella Faring

Dick Powell's Zane Grey Theater (1961) (CBS) "One Must Die" ... Sarah/Melanie Davidson

The Foxes (1961) ... Millicent Fox

Route 66 (1963) (CBS) "Same Picture, Different Frame" ... Morgan Harper

Della (1965) (TV Movie) AKA Fatal Confinement ... Della Chappell

The Man From U.N.C.L.E (1967) (NBC) "The Karate Killers" or "The Five Daughters Affair" ... Amanda True

The Lucy Show (1968) (CBS) "Lucy and Joan Crawford" or "The Lost Star" ... Herself

The Secret Storm (1968) (CBS) (daytime soap opera) ... Joan Boreman Kane #2 (temporary replacement for Christina Crawford)

Night Gallery (1969) (NBC) "Eyes" ... Claudia Menlo

The Virginian (1970) (NBC) "The Nightmare" ... Stephanie White

Beyond the Water's Edge (1972) (TV Movie) ... Allison Hayes

The Sixth Sense (1972) (ABC) "Dear Joan: We're Going To Scare You To Death!" ... Joan Fairchild

Archive Footage

Four Days in November (1964) ... Herself (signs autographs)

MGM's Big Parade of Comedy (1964) ... Herself

That's Entertainment (1974) ... Herself

That's Dancing (1985) ... Herself

sources

What Ever Happened to Mommie Dearest?

""If you've earned a position, be proud of it. Don't hide it. I want to be recognized."

- Joan Crawford

Bibliography

Selected Source Material

A number of books, magazines, newspapers, documentaries and interviews, as well as the films themselves provided sources of information and factual data that went into the writing of this book. Thank you to the many sources referenced throughout the book. There were many individuals whose work, insights, reviews, comments and suggestions that also helped make this book possible.

Books

Brett, David. *Joan Crawford: Hollywood Martyr*. 2006. Da Capo Press.

Castle, William. *Step Right Up! I'm Gonna Scare the Pants off America*. 1992. Pharos Books.

Chandler, Charlotte. *Not the Girl Next Door*. 2008. Simon and Schuster.

Considine, Shaun. *Bette & Joan: The Divine Feud*. 1989. Dell Publishing.

Cowie, Peter. *Joan Crawford: The Enduring Star*. 2009. Rizzoli International Publications.

Crawford, Joan. *Portrait of Joan*. 1962. Doubleday.

Crawford, Joan. *My Way of Life*. 1971. Simon and Schuster.

Davis, Bette. *The Lonely Life*. 1962. G.P. Putnam's Sons.

Davis, Bette. *This 'n That*. 1987. Putnam Publishing Group.

Eames, John Douglas. *The MGM Story*. 1989. Portland House.

Finler, Joel. *The Hollywood Story*. 1988. Crown Publishers.

Guiles, Fred Lawrence. *Joan Crawford: The Last Word*. 1995. Birch Lane Press.

Hirschhorn, Clive. *The Universal Story*. 1983. Crown Publishers.

Johnes, Carl. *Crawford: The Last Years*. 1979. Dell Publishing.

McCarty, John. *Psychos: Eighty Years of Mad Movies, Maniacs, and Murderous Deeds*. 1986. St Martin's Press.

McCarty, John. *The Fearmakers*. 1994. St. Martin's Press.

Newquist, Roy. *Conversations With Joan Crawford*. 1980. Citadel Press.

Parish, James Robert. *The Hollywood Book of Death*. 2001. McGraw-Hill.

Quirk, Lawrence J. and Schoell. *Joan Crawford: The Essential Biography*. 2002. The University Press of Kentucky.

Quirk, Lawrence J. *The Films of Joan Crawford*. 1971. Citadel Press.

Schoell, William. *Stay Out of the Shower*. 1985. Dembner Books.

Shelley, Peter. *Grand Dame Guignol Cinema*. 2009. McFarland & Company.

Skal, David. *The Monster Show*. 1993. Penguin Books.

Spada, James. *More Than a Woman*. 1993. Bantam Books.

Spoto, Donald. *Possessed*. 2010. Morrow/HarperCollins Books.

Stallings, Penny. *Flesh and Fantasy*. 1978. St. Martin's Press.

Thomas, Bob. *Joan Crawford*. 1978. Bantam Books.

Wayne, Jane Ellen. *Crawford's Men*. 1988. Prentice Hall Press.
Wilkerson, Tichi and Borie, Marcia. *Hollywood Legends*. 1988. Tale Weaver Publishing.

Magazines, Newspapers and Transcripts

Baker, Phil. "Joan Crawford: The Last Word Book Review." *Sunday Times*. April 7, 1996.

Barson, Michael. "From Hackwork to Highbrow Horror." *The New York Times*. August 13, 1995.

Cagle, Jess. "Joan Crawford: The Mildred Pierce Actress Saved Her Best Performance for Oscar Night." *Entertainment Weekly*. March, 1996.

Eddy, Steve. "B-Movie Director Castle Looks Back in 'Step Right Up'." *The Orange County Register*. April 12, 1992.

Jackson, Kevin. "They Came from Beyond The Pale: Matinees Shamelessly Vulgar Hero is a Grade Z Horror Movie Producer of the 60s. But Which One?" *The Independent*. June 11, 1993.

Maslin, Janet. "There's a Horror Movie in Here!" *The New York Times*. January 29, 1993.

Price, Michael H. "Moviemaker Revisits His 60s Fright-Film Salad Days in "Matinee'." *Star Tribune*. February 13, 1993.

Staff. "The Gimmicks of William Castle." *The Times-Picayune*. February 6, 1993.

Staff. "Obituary: William Castle, 63, Movie Producer." *The New York Times*. June 2, 1977.

Thompson, Howard. "Thriller Double Bill." *The New York Times*. July 22, 1965.

Internet Sources

The Internet Movie Database, www.imdb.com

Wikipedia, www.wikipedia.org

The Numbers – Box Office Data, Movie Stars, Idle Speculation, www.the-numbers.com

Box Office Mojo, www.boxofficemojo.com

What Ever Happened to Mommie Dearest?

index

.

Index

J

K

L

S

T

What Ever Happened to Mommie Dearest?

What Ever Happened to Mommie Dearest?

Photographic Credits

In addition to the selected bibliograpy of sources we would also like to acknowledge the many photographs used in this book. While many are part of the author's private collection, we would like to specifically acknowledge the following for illustrations used that are used for the purpose of review to highlight and complement the text:

20th Century Fox, Warner Bros., Columbia, Universal, Life Magazine, Cinema Photos, CinemaShop.

What Ever Happened to Mommie Dearest?

What Ever Happened to Mommie Dearest?

About the Author

J ohn William Law is a writer and journalist whose work has appeared in newspapers, magazines and books. He has worked on the staffs of daily, weekly and monthly publications. He is the author of numerous books and narrates a podcast on iTunes entitled *The Movie Files*. He has appeared on television and film documentaries discussing film history and on national public radio. He lives in San Francisco. His book *Alfred Hitchcock: The Icon Years* received the Best Biography Readers Favorite Book Award for non-fiction in 2011. His books include:

Curse of the Silver Screen - Tragedy & Disaster Behind the Movies (1999, Aplomb Publishing)

Scare Tactic - The Life and Films of William Castle (2000, Writers Club Press)

Reel Horror - True Horrors Behind Hollywood's Scary Movies (2004, Aplomb Publishing)

Master of Disaster: Irwin Allen - The Disaster Years (2008, Aplomb Publishing)

Alfred Hitchcock: The Icon Years (2010, Aplomb Publishing)

Death of a Pop Star: Tragic Endings of Pop & Rock Music Icons (2011, Aplomb Publishing

If you enjoyed this book, you might also enjoy *Alfred Hitchcock: The Icon Years*. Published by Aplomb Publishing, the book received the Readers Favorite Book Award for Best Non-Fiction: Biography in 2011. It is available from our Web site at www.aplombpublishing.com or from major booksellers and Amazon.com.

CPSIA information can be obtained
at www.ICGtesting.com
Printed in the USA
BVHW052310261222
655035BV00009B/212